D1282966

MODERN BRITISH
LYRICS

MODERN
BRITISH LYRICS

An Anthology
COMPILED BY
STANTON A. COBLENTZ

Granger Index Reprint Series

BOOKS FOR LIBRARIES PRESS
FREEPORT, NEW YORK

First Published 1925
Reprinted 1972

INTERNATIONAL STANDARD BOOK NUMBER:
0-8369-6328-8

LIBRARY OF CONGRESS CATALOG CARD NUMBER:
70-38596

PRINTED IN THE UNITED STATES OF AMERICA
BY
NEW WORLD BOOK MANUFACTURING CO., INC.
HALLANDALE, FLORIDA 33009

PREFACE

There are two obvious ways of compiling an anthology of verse. The first is to confine one's self primarily to the more popular works of the more popular writers; the second is to disregard names and reputations alike in the search for poems that will shine by their own inherent qualities. In the case of compilations covering material that has repeatedly been sifted and re-sifted, the former method will perhaps prove advantageous; in the case of compilations invading virgin or relatively untrodden areas, the latter system alone can be expected to yield results. And it is this plan, accordingly, which I have attempted to follow in "Modern British Lyrics." As in my American anthology, I have been guided by the realization that the contemporary field is still largely in a state of critical chaos; that the authentic pearls and diamonds have yet to be sorted out from the gems of paste and glass; that a large quantity of noteworthy work must inevitably escape notice amid the continuous inundations of the written word; and that too often an author will flare into prominence merely by accident or by a meretricious appeal to the taste of a moment while others of more solid merit must sing in loneliness and obscurity.

For this reason, I have endeavored to make "Modern British Lyrics" representative less of those poets whose names are on every one's tongue than of their more numerous fellows who are heard only as voices in the wilderness. While I have not gone to the fatuous extent of excluding any writer simply because he is well known, I have striven not to emphasize that which is no longer in need of emphasis; I have aimed to consider the poem first and the name of the author afterwards if at all; I have sought at all times to avoid the great pitfall of the anthologist—the error of mere reduplication, of a barren republication of that which has already been abundantly made public. If in some few cases I have felt an irresistible attraction for poems that have previously appeared in anthologies, yet in general I have attempted to strike out for the trackless spaces, for the hidden byways and treasure caves of poetry, and so to bring before the American public the work of deserving British poets that might otherwise have escaped attention.

In this project I have been actuated throughout by a definite principle of selection. As the title of the anthology implies, I have restricted my choice to poems with a lyrical element; and, as in "Modern American Lyrics," I have confined myself to verse in the traditional forms and meters, making the quality of music the primary technical test of the poetic. But since the *vers libre* movement has taken root less firmly in Great Britain than in

America, and since the innovators in form and in particular the eccentrics are less conspicuous abroad, the lyric basis of the selection need not be emphasized as in the case of the American compilation; and I may limit myself to explaining that certain dramatic and narrative poets of distinction, and even some ostensible lyricists of reputation, have been excluded because their work has not that singing strain which has been the hallmark of every notable lyric writer from Sappho to Francis Ledwidge and Walter de la Mare.

Aside from the restrictions as to form and musical quality, the question of inclusion and exclusion has necessarily been largely a matter of individual discretion. Because of the size of the field, I have been compelled to confine my selections to the British Isles; because of my desire to make the volume essentially contemporary, I have given the preference to living poets or to those who might be living but for a premature death on the battlefield; and because the unexplored spaces are so wide, the darkness still so unsounded, I have perhaps had to yield occasionally to mere groping chance, and by inadvertence may have neglected poets quite as worthy of recognition as any that are represented. The restrictions of copyright, moreover, have played their ironclad and unfortunate part in the elimination of certain writers, and even in the omission of desirable poems by those whose names grace the table of contents.

S. A. C.

New York, June, 1925.

CONTENTS

MODERN BRITISH
LYRICS

TO-DAY

Alone To-day stands in the sun.
—Why dream they, who their race must run?
—Between two precipices steep
To-day arises from the deep.

Athwart the deep abyss of night
It stretches like a ribbon bright,

Between the dawn and dusk it lies,
Apex of two eternities:

To-morrow dim and yesterday
Are lost within that twilight grey,

Only a slender patch of light
Between the double jaws of night,
While the full glory of the sun
Proclaims To-day the only one.

Everest Lewin.

THE IDEAL

The night is dark and warm and very still,
  Only the moon goes pallid and alone;
The moon and I the whole wide heavens fill,
  And all the earth lies little, lost, unknown.

I walk along the byways of my Soul,
  Beyond the streets where all the world may go,
Until at last I reach the hidden goal
  Built up in strength where only I may know.

For in my Soul a temple have I made,
  Set on a height, divine and steep and far,
Nor often may I hope those floors to tread,
  Or reach the gates that glimmer like a star.

O secret, inner shining of my dream,
  How clear thou risest on my soul to-night!
Forth will I fare and seek the heavenly beam,
  And stand within the precincts of the light.

And I will press beyond the curtain'd door,
  And up the empty aisle where no one sings;
There will I fall before thee and adore,
  And feel the shadowy winnowing of thy wings.

2

So will I reach thee, Spirit; for I have known
   Thy voice, and looked upon thy blinding eyes,
And well thou knowest the world to me is grown
   One dimness whence thy dreamy beacons rise.

Nor ask I any hope nor any end,
   That thus for thee I dream all day, all night;
But, like the moon along the skies, I wend,
   Knowing no world below my borrowed light.

                A. Mary F. Robinson.

THE SAIL

To-day it is as though the rain
Had no beginning in the sky,
Nor touched the earth with its fine train
But like a spectre slanted by.

A spectre that the lost wind blows
To errantries that shape its own,
And like a sail it swells and goes,
And like a sail the wind is blown.

The hulls their ancient moorings slip,
Thick ropes of mist the old woods trail,
Earth moves, a ghostly-timbered ship,
Behind that urgent, sweeping sail.

And some perceiving wraith am I,
Who watch from a forgotten strand
The shrouded ship of time sail by—
A spectral sail in sole command.

Cyril G. Taylor.

VISIONS

When in the blue dusk of a summer night
  I watch God's largess of His silver stars,
  Sometimes, it seems, the adamantine bars
Fall from the tall gates of the Infinite;
And Time stands waiting. Then I seem to hear,
  As one that listens from a lonely height
  To waters breaking on an unknown sea,
The strong pulse of the world-heart throbbing near;
The mists roll back, and for a space stand clear
  The great white windows of eternity.

William Noel Hodgson.

A VISION OF BEAUTY

Where we sat at dawn together, while the star-rich
    heavens shifted,
We were weaving dreams in silence, suddenly the
    veil was lifted.
By a hand of fire awakened, in a moment caught
    and led
Upward to the heaven of heavens—through the
    star-mists overhead
Flare and flaunt the monstrous highlands; on the
    sapphire coast of night
Fall the ghostly froth and fringes of the ocean of
    the light.
Many-colored shine the vapors: to the moon-eye far
    away
'Tis the fairy ring of twilight, mid the spheres of
    night and day,
Girdling with a rainbow cincture round the planet
    where we go,
We and it together fleeting, poised upon the pearly
    glow;
We and it and all together flashing through the
    starry spaces
In a tempest dream of beauty lighting up the face
    of faces.

Half our eyes behold the glory; half within the
spirit's glow
Echoes of the noiseless revels and the will of Beauty
go.
By a hand of fire uplifted—to her star-strewn
palace brought,
To the mystic heart of beauty and the secret of her
thought:
Here of yore the ancient Mother in the fire mists
sank to rest,
And she built her dreams about her, rayed from out
her burning breast:
Here the wild will woke within her lighting up her
flying dreams,
Round and round the planets whirling break in
woods and flowers and streams,
And the winds are shaken from them as the leaves
from off the rose,
And the feet of earth go dancing in the way that
beauty goes,
And the souls of earth are kindled by the incense
of her breath
As her light alternate lures them through the gates
of birtn and death.
O'er the fields of space together following her flying
traces,
In a radiant tumult thronging, suns and stars and
myriad races
Mount the spirit spires of beauty, reaching onward
to the day

7

When the Shepherd of the Ages draws his misty
    hordes away
Through the glimmering deeps to silence, and within
    the awful fold
Life and love and joy forever vanish as a tale is
    told,
Lost within the Mother's being. So the vision
    flamed and fled,
And before the glory fallen every other dream lay
    dead.

                                        A. E.

THE TRAVELLERS

A strange procession passes still
Across the valley, up the hill,
Setting a fringe upon the day,
Where the path lies a little way
Along the bare and windy heights;—
A fringe that wavers all day long,
Uncertain as the Northern Lights
When days are short and frosts are strong.

Here at my window as I sit
Watching the changing figures flit,
I hear the fly upon the pane,
The sweet birds singing after rain,
But never any sound at all
From those mysterious travellers,
No voices harsh or musical
Upon that silent way of theirs.

They never turn or pause to rest,
But onward to the shining West,
Like some swart serpent, fold on fold,
The long procession still is rolled.
But where they go, or what they seek,
Unguessed beyond the mountain lies;

I see them slowly gain the peak,
And slowly vanish from my eyes.

Where the blue heavens touch the hill,—
Shade after shadow moving still.
Yet sometimes in my dreams I pass
With them across the meadow grass,
And up the purple mountain side,
Until the long bare ridge I gain,
And see before me, stretching wide
Between the hills, a quiet plain,

All beautiful with shady trees,
And gardens, where the drowsy bees
Make music in the ear of sleep.
I see a broad, blue river sweep
By banks where the wild roses dream,
And swans and water-lilies sway
With the slow rhythm of the stream
Above their shadows, white as they;

And where the trees most shady are,
A city, shining like a star.
The river laves her marble quays,
All marble are her palaces;
The white rose in her garden flowers,
And milk-white are the doves that fly
About the gleaming marble towers.
Then from my longing heart a cry

Breaks forth,—and all my dream is gone,
Shattered and lost and overthrown.

But still my heart with longing stirs
To join those silent travellers;
And still I watch them day by day,
That strange procession passing still
Silent upon its westward way
Across the valley, up the hill.

And in my heart full well I know
I, too, at last shall rise and go
To seek within the shining West
That city of eternal rest.

Duncan J. Robertson.

IMMORTALITY

I

When other beauty governs other lips,
   And snowdrops come to strange and happy
      springs,
When seas renewed bear yet unbuilded ships,
   And alien hearts know all familiar things,
When frosty nights bring comrades to enjoy
   Sweet hours at hearths where we no longer sit,
When Liverpool is one with dusty Troy,
   And London famed as Attica for wit. . . .
How shall it be with you, and you, and you,
   How with us all who have gone greatly here
In friendship, making some delight, some true
   Song in the dark, some story against fear?
Shall song still walk with love, and life be brave,
And we, who were all these, be but the grave?

II

No; lovers yet shall tell the nightingale
   Sometimes a song that we of old time made,
And gossips gathered at the twilight ale
   Shall say, "These two were friends," or, "Un-
      afraid

12

"Of bitter thought were those because they loved
  "Better than most." And sometimes shall be told
How one, who died in his young beauty, moved,
  As Astrophel, those English hearts of old.
And the new seas shall take the new ships home
  Telling how yet the Dymock orchards stand,
And you shall walk with Julius at Rome,
  And Paul shall be my fellow in the strand;
There in the midst of all those words shall be
Our names, our ghosts, our immortality.

John Drinkwater.

SONNET

It may be that beyond our mortal view
In a great factory on the outer verge
Of outer heaven, a heavenly Demiurge
Through the long ages shapes the earth anew.
Perchance hereafter he shall raise his head
Having fulfilled his task, while all about
The lamps of the old Universe burn out
And daylight waxes in the darkened shed.
Then rising from his toil he shall fling wide
The Workshop doors, and quench the lights
    that lurk
In windless corners, and his labour done,
Shall stand upon the threshold satisfied,
Beholding the new world, his handiwork,
All-glorious beneath the risen sun.

Roger Heath.

REFLECTIONS

How often have I gazed with upturned face
And wondered at the miracle of night,
That vast immeasurable vault of light,
And marvelled at the swift unending race
Of blazing suns and stars aloft in space,
Yet knew behind them all there watched a might,
A power which ordered and controlled their flight;
And even this small earth could mark and trace.

When I consider this infinity
A nameless terror clutches at my soul,
Thinking of one whose unperturbed eyes
These myriad, myriad stars of ours can see,
And knows them fragments of a mighty whole,
A little light in the eternal skies.

W. A. Lee.

RHAPSODY

As when trees are shrouded in December
Men recall the perfumes of the flower-time,
So we sing a life we half remember:—
How we heard in some primeval shower-time
Liquid song of rain upon blue rivers:
Dreamed on isles in windless oceans planted
Where a dim green twilight bird enchanted
Under domes of drooping leafage quivers:
How we climbed, on many a hidden planet,
Eagle-heights stirred by a starry breeze:
Watched by coffined kings in tombs of granite
Where the darkness hangs like boughs of trees,
Glimpsing in the reddening light of torches
Ghosts of sombre vaults and looming porches,
Cyclopean faces, giant knees:
How we anchored in a violet haven,
Seeking under light of unknown stars
Mountains paler than the moonlight, graven
Into shapes of pinnacles and scars:
Where our boat set all the lilies swinging
Sailed up rivers hushed and leafy-arboured
And, in caves of hanging blossom harboured,
Heard the sound of an immortal singing.

16

As when breathed upon, the ashen ember
Blossoms into fire again and fades,
So bright Junes flame up through our December
And at random whiles we half remember
Sudden gusts of an immortal singing,
Ancient visions of remote crusades.

Martin Armstrong.

BEAUTY

I sought for beauty in forgetfulness
Of the harsh days, the mean and bitter hours,
The eyes wherein a shrinking spirit cowers,
The broken hearts, the forms of drab distress;
I sought her in strange books where legends press
In rich profusion, in the scent of flowers,
Bird song and starlight, wooing the high powers
For sense and certainty of her caress.

I found her not. Immortally diffused,
No bloom or light or sound can prison her,
No drug of legend make her wholly mine;
She haunts the ruined hours, the lives abused,
Distils her silence in the city's stir,
And pours out sorrow as a golden wine.

William Kean Seymour.

THE SNARE

Far away and long ago
This trouble at my heart began:
Ere Eden perished like a flower,
Or Eve had shed her tears an hour,
Or Adam knew himself a man,
In every leaf of every tree
Beauty had set a snare for me.

Far away and long ago
Her loveliest song began to chime.
Bright Hector fell, and at the stroke
Ten thousand hearts like mine awoke
In every age and every clime.
She stood bestriding Time and Space
Amid the stars, and lit the rose
With scent and color, and she chose
My country for a dwelling place,
And set a snare in every tree
Awaiting me, awaiting me!

Edward Davison.

BARCAROLLE

Dark Hesper climbs the evening sky
   And sails grow dim on rosy seas
And golden in the west there lie
   The Isles of the Hesperides.

The Night across the still lagoon
   Floats in her purple gondola
And like a fairy ship the moon
   Sails, with a single Pilot-star.

The water laps the languid oar,
   Ripples and gurgles, croons and sings;
Low through the dusk a troubadour
   Murmurs his love to muted strings.

The clinging darkness wraps us round,
   More tender grows the fragrant breeze:
Shall not our own sweet isles be found
   The Isles of the Hesperides?

S. Matthewman.

IMMORTALITY

One star upon the desert of the sky,
  One song upon the silences of night,
  Upon the tossing of the stream, one light,
One moment in a blank eternity.

For, O my love, eternity is drear,
  And soon we both shall weary of it so,
That we shall turn and hide ourselves for fear
  In that sweet hour God gave us long ago.

We cannot wander from it very far,
  For down the long wild ways, it calls us home,
Red through the evening like a fallen star,
  A dim undying hearth for loves that roam.

I feel were I to meet you I might not
  Even know you in the street, nor you know me—
  You might look back and whisper, 'Who is she?'
And I might sigh at something half forgot.

But in our Moment I can kiss your face,
  Smiling and strong—unchanged by all the years;
And I can hold you there a little space,
  And you hold me—unchanged by all my tears.

And I can whisper to you of that night
  When our dark boat made moon-swept waters
    hiss.
  Your face was wet with spray, spray-white your
    kiss,
Your eyes were stars that I had set alight.

Dim planets hung above the trembling trees,
  The suck of water shook the misty air,
  The darkness showed you magic in my hair,
The darkness showed you rest upon my knees.

We saw two wandering stars fall through the sky—
  'Twas you and I, lost in the chilly haze,
  Apart, adrift, forsaken, but ablaze
With one short hour's eternal ecstasy.

And into our poor love of rags and tears
  The fire of life and deathless love rushed down,
Rushed the great love of this world's million years,
  Gave us the kingdom, set on us the crown—

Gave us all love of lovers since the morn
  Of love in the dim daybreak of the earth,
  Gave us all harmonies since music's birth,
Gave us all colours since the first red dawn—

Gave us the springtime with its changing tunes,
Gave us the mysteries of many Junes,
Gave us the stars, gave us the trackless sea,
Gave us each other to eternity.

Love may be gone, as you are gone, my dear,
　　But our almighty moment cannot die—
It shall stand fast when the last crumbling sphere
　　Shall crash out of the ruin of the sky.

When the last constellations faint and fall,
　　When the last planets burst in fiery foam,
When all the winds have sunk asleep, when all
　　The worn way-weary comets have come home—

When past and present and the future flee,
　　My moment lives! and I shall hold you there.
It lives to be my immortality,
　　An immortality which you shall share.

One star upon the desert of the sky,
　　One song upon the silences of night,
　　Upon the tossing of the stream, one light,
One moment in a blank eternity.

Sheila Kaye-Smith

TO MY MOTHER

At evening when the twilight curtains fall,
Before the lamps are lit within my room,
My memories hang bright upon the gloom,
Like ancient frescoes painted on the wall.

And I can hear the call of birds and bells
And shadowy sound of waves, and wind through
    leaves
And wind that rustles through the burnished
    sheaves,
And far off voices whispering farewells.

I dream again the joy I used to know
While straying by the sea that hardly sighed
A sorrow in my singing, as the tide
Crept up to clasp me, smiled, and let me go.

And I remember all the glad lost hours,
The racing of brown rabbits on the hill,
The winds that prowled around the lonely mill,
Laburnum laughter, music of the flowers.

The berries plucked with loitering delight,
Staining the dusk with purple, till the thought

24

Of starry little ghosts behind us caught
Our hearts and made us fearful of the night.

The London evenings huddled in the rain
Whose misty prisms shone with lamplight pale,
Making our hearts seem sinister and frail,
Fainting our thoughts with mystery and pain.

I have a world of memories to dream,
To touch with loving fingers as a sigh
Revives a little flame and lets it die.
Ah, were the days as lovely as they seem

Now that they look so peaceful lying dead?
And is it all the hope of Joy we have,
The broken trophies of the things she gave
And took away to give us dreams instead?

The things we love and lose before we find
The way to love them well enough and keep,
That now are woven on the looms of sleep,
That now are only music on the wind.

Iris Tree.

TO A DISTANT ONE

Through wild by-ways I come to you, my love,
Nor ask of those I meet the surest way,
What way I turn I cannot go astray
And miss you in my life. Though Fate may prove
A tardy guide she will not make delay
Leading me through strange seas and distant lands,
I'm coming still, though slowly, to your hands.
        We'll meet one day.

There is so much to do, so little done,
In my life's space that I perforce did leave
Love at the moonlit-trysting place to grieve
Till fame and other little things were won.
I have missed much that I shall not retrieve,
Far will I wander yet with much to do.
Much will I spurn before I yet meet you,
        So fair I can't deceive.

Your name is in the whisper of the woods
Like Beauty calling for a poet's song
To one whose harp has suffered many a wrong
In the lean hands of Pan. And when the broods
Of flower eyes waken all the streams along
In tender whiles, I feel most near to you:—
Oh, when we meet there shall be sun and blue
        Strong as the spring is strong.

Francis Ledwidge.

WAITING

Every day you do not come
A little bit of summer dies,
A rose-leaf flutters from a rose;
With less expectant eyes,

Every day you do not come,
A blackbird from some lofty spray
Watches another sunset fade
And sings his heart away.

Every day you do not come
Some clinging tendril is untwined;
The sweetness of the heliotrope
Is wasted on the wind.

Every day you do not come
A little later wakes the dawn,
A little sooner steals the dusk
Across the shadowed lawn.

Helen E. Holland.

WOMAN'S SONG

No more upon my bosom rest thee,
Too often have my hands caressed thee,
   My lips thou knowest well, too well;
Lean to my heart no more thine ear
My spirit's living truth to hear—
   —It has no more to tell.

In what dark hour, in what strange night,
Burnt to the butt the candle's light
   That lit our room so long?
I do not know, I thought I knew
How love could be both sweet and true:
   I also thought it strong.

Where has the flame departed? Where,
Amid the empty wastes of air,
   Is that which dwelt with us?
Was it a fancy? Did we make
Only a show for dead love's sake,
   It being so piteous?

No more against my bosom press thee,
Seek no more that my hands caress thee,
   Leave the sad lips thou hast known so well;
If to my heart thou lean thine ear,
There grieving thou shalt only hear
   Vain murmuring of an empty shell.

Edward Shanks.

TO MY BELOVED DEAD

I

In the profound and dreadful calm of night,
Worn with the newness of my grief, I come
Dry-eyed, and fall beside you, spent and dumb,
Dreading the dawn, with all its aching light;

Dreading the day, and all it holds for me
Of restlessness and forms that come and go;
New things to do, new things to see and know,
That were not yet, when you were there to see;

And shut my eyes, and for a while pretend
That I can lean against you, feel your hand,
Hear your heart beat, and know you understand,
Though you are farther than the wide world's end.

Ah! My Belovèd, swiftly, silently,
Surely your kind, kind ghost shall comfort me.

II

It cannot be that you shall no more come
Radiant with laughter, holding hands for mine,
Seeking my soul for Love's most earnest sign,
Meeting my thought with eloquent thought and
    dumb.

29

It cannot be that I must look for you
There, where the Summer flames, and find you not;
Of splendid sunsets know you all forgot,
Nor find you in the rain, nor the sky's blue.

For here the lily all her sweetness yields,
And all my heart is open to the sun;
And, seeking peace in grief, the long day done,
I find it in the silver, moonlit fields.

Then, by the beauty of the world I know
That you are here, and will not let me go.

Ethel Ashton Edwards.

THE RETURN

Far, through the quiet night, my Loved One came;
 He said: "I have come back to you awhile,"
And called me by a most belovèd name;
 He held me in his arms, I saw him smile . . .
"We had too little time together, Love,
 And so I have come back" . . . I held him close;
The inviolate night broke on us from above,
 And sheltered us in darkness and repose.

I feared to break the silence, lest the spell
 Of that great happiness were broken too.
We neither spoke: there was no word to tell
 In language what we held so wholly true . . .

There came a gleam of silver from the lawn . . .
I woke . . . I lay alone . . . and it was Dawn.

Ethel Ashton Edwards.

31

THE TRYST

I

She will return, as surely as the morn:
Death cannot hold her, nor the grave immure,
Nor hope of saintly paradises lure
To leave her love upon the world forlorn.
But whispers on the early breezes borne
Will voice her gladness; she will keep her way
Across the stillness of the middle day,
And all her beauty by the night be worn.

Joy as of old in her melodious moods,
Who is made one with universal things,
Will be his stay. And if to him she brings
Her human sorrow in the rain, and broods
Over the autumn magic of the woods,
In such full griefs there is no room for pain,
But wonder and the touch of peace again,
And trysting in the haunted solitudes.

II

Ah would that he might know the gentle way
Death has with Love! Nor call his darling dead;
Nor grieve that all his dear delight is fled

In starry new forgetful paths to stray;
But in the precincts of the fretful day
And through the peopled darkness be aware
Of me, among the unseen watchers there.
All else is granted. This alone I pray.

The garden of his heart with sun and shower
I will besiege: my being shall renew
The bloom of spring in every avenue,
And move the languid air with a fresh power
Of love, and shake each wind-awakened flower
To murmur many a soft enchanted word
In falling petals. Surely they will be heard,
Nor his soul fail me at the trysting hour.

E. V. Rieu.

ELEGY

The wood is bare: a river-mist is steeping
   The trees that winter's chill of life bereaves:
Only their stiffened boughs break silence, weeping
    Over their fallen leaves;

That lie upon the dank earth brown and rotten,
   Miry and matted in the soaking wet:
Forgotten with the spring, that is forgotten
    By them that can forget.

Yet it was here we walked when ferns were spring-
       ing,
   And through the mossy bank shot bud and
       blade:—
Here found in summer, when the birds were singing,
    A green and pleasant shade.

'Twas here we loved in sunnier days and greener;
   And now, in this disconsolate decay,
I come to see her where I most have seen her,
    And touch the happier day.

For on this path, at every turn and corner,
   The fancy of her figure on me falls:
Yet walks she with the slow step of a mourner,
    Nor hears my voice that calls.

So through my heart there winds a track of feeling,
  A path of memory, that is all her own:
Whereto her phantom beauty ever stealing
    Haunts the sad spot alone.

About her steps the trunks are bare, the branches
  Drip heavy tears upon her downcast head;
And bleed from unseen wounds that no sun
    staunches,
    For the year's sun is dead.

And dead leaves wrap the fruits that summer
    planted;
  And birds that love the South have taken wing.
The wanderer, loitering o'er the scene enchanted,
    Weeps, and despairs of spring.

                                    Robert Bridges.

THE DARKLING THRUSH

I leant upon a coppice gate
  When Frost was spectre-gray,
And Winter's dregs made desolate
  The weakening eye of day.
The tangled bine-stems scored the sky
  Like strings of broken lyres,
And all mankind that haunted nigh
  Had sought their household fires.

The land's sharp features seemed to be
  The Century's corpse outleant,
His crypt the cloudy canopy,
  The wind his death-lament.
The ancient pulse of germ and birth
  Was shrunken hard and dry,
And every spirit upon earth
  Seemed fervorless as I.

At once a voice arose among
  The bleak twigs overhead
In a full-hearted evensong
  Of joy illimited;
An aged thrush, frail, gaunt, and small,
  In blast-beruffled plume,

Had chosen thus to fling his soul
  Upon the growing gloom.

So little cause for carollings
  Of such ecstatic sound
Was written on terrestrial things
  Afar or nigh around,
That I could think there trembled through
  His happy good-night air
Some blessed Hope, whereof he knew
  And I was unaware.

Thomas Hardy.

THE STARLING

A starling whistles from the chimney pot
And all my world, as by some magic spell,
Is touched to loveliness: now quite forgot
Are the drab streets; I see a dell
Where happy wild things play, the honey bees,
Rabbits with startled eyes and listening ears,
Scared by the smallest whisper of the breeze
That laughs among the grasses at their fears;
Blue butterflies, like scraps of the blue sky,
Flit to and fro, and with the singing stream
A merry water-wagtail hurries by.
O lovely ways, and are they but a dream!
Sweet feathered conjuror, must my senses wake!
Pipe on, lest this too tired heart should break.

E. Joyce Harrison.

ON THE WESTERN CLIFFS

Out of the windy waste
  Of waters rolling gray,
Homeward the red sails haste
  Across the bay.
Over the downs I see
  The summits black and sheer,
When evening on the lea
  Is pale and clear.

There as the twilight falls,
  The seabirds float and cry;
—Only the mountain walls
  Make faint reply;—
Or with broad wing decline
  Down to their rocky home,
Warm in the chilly brine,
  Nestled in foam.

Over the oozy weed
  The flying feet haste on,
Hither and thither speed
  Ere day be done.
For them the fry that dive
  Poise in their liquid bed,

They neither fear nor strive,
  Sleep and are fed.

Then comes the night, the end,
  What should their dying be?
Death steals, a silent friend,
  Out of the sea.
Under the rocky edge
  They close their languid eye,
While shrill from tuft and ledge
  Their brethren cry.

Or where the stranded wrack,
  Rimmed on the stunted grass,
Rattles so dry and black
  As the winds pass,
The draggled feather flies,
  The frail denuded bones
Bleach, and the sightless eyes,
  On the gray stones.

Under the weary hill
  The wandering footsteps cease;
He that must wander still
  Envies your peace.
Wasted by harsh events,
  Sighs to be large and free,
Mix with the elements,
  And breathe, and be.

Arthur Christopher Benson.

THE ROCK POOL

This is the sea. In these uneven walls
   A wave lies prisoned. Far and far away
Outward to ocean, as the slow tide falls,
   Her sisters through the capes that hold the bay
Dancing in lovely liberty recede.
   Yet lovely in captivity she lies,
Filled with soft colours, where the wavering weed
   Moves gently and discloses to our eyes
Blurred shining veins of rock and lucent shells
   Under the light-shot water; and here repose
Small quiet fish and dimly glowing bells
   Of sleeping sea-anemonies that close
Their tender fronds and will not now awake
Till on these rocks the waves returning break.

Edward Shanks.

THE ANCIENT MOTHER

Thou art the mother of all things, O Sea,
From out whose teeming, pulsing womb once crept
The life primordial, when green earth yet slept.
How shall we sing, we that are born of thee,
Thy age-old saga of maternity?
We are rebellious children: thou hast leapt
To snatch our lives again and we have wept
And cried to heaven of thy treachery.

Yet still thine ancient beauties must we praise:
The cries of birds in oceans many-isled,
The strange sea-gardens, where the pale weed
    sways;
The taste of salt on breezes undefiled,
And surf-artillery along the bays—
O mother-sea, I also am thy child!

Margaret S. Dangerfield.

SEA-MADNESS

I cannot stay in any inland place,
  The sea-song drowns the beating of my blood.
I find no joy in any woman's face,
  My sole desire is the sea's grey flood.
With eager arms I clasp the bitter wave
  That will not wait to quench my maddening fire;
But laughs,—and passing spurns her pleading slave
  Who burns unceasingly with sick desire.
Wave-buffeted and belled with glistening foam,
  Eyes blinded, and lips stinging from her kiss,
I stand, whose sea-born madness makes me roam
  Homeless where surging waters crash and hiss.
No power may cure this longing for the wave
'Till her cold bosom makes my restless grave.

                    Periwinkle Cotgrave.

43

THE VOICE OF THE WATERS

Where the Greyhound River windeth through a
  loneliness so deep,
Scarce a wild fowl shakes the quiet that the purple
  boglands keep,
Only God exults in silence over fields no man may
  reap.

Where the silver wave with sweetness fed the tiny
  lives of grass
I was bent above, my image mirrored in the fleeting
  glass,
And a voice from out the water through my being
  seemed to pass.

"Still above the waters brooding, spirit, in thy time-
  less quest;
Was the glory of thine image trembling over east
  and west
Not divine enough when mirrored in the morning
  water's breast?"

With the sighing voice that murmured I was borne
  to ages dim
Ere the void was lit by beauty breathed upon by
  seraphim,

We were cradled there together folded in the peace
    in Him.

One to be the master spirit, one to be the slave
    awoke,
One to shape itself obedient to the fiery words we
    spoke,
Flame and flood and stars and mountains from the
    primal waters broke.

I was huddled in the heather when the vision failed
    its light,
Still and blue and vast above me towered aloft the
    solemn height,
Where the stars like dewdrops glistened on the
    mountain slope of night.

A. E.

FIRE-FLIES

I

To-night I watch the fire-flies rise
  And shine along the air;
They float beneath the starry skies,
  As mystical and fair,
Over the hedge where dimly glows
The deep gold of the Persian rose.

I watch the fire-flies drift and float,
  Each is a dreamy flame,
Star-colored each, a starry mote,
  Like stars not all the same;
But whiter some, or faintly green.
Or warmest blue was ever seen.

They cross and cross and disappear,
  And then again they glow;
Still drifting faintly there and here,
  Still crossing to and fro,
As though in all their wandering
They wove a wide and shining thing.

II

O fire-flies, would I knew the weft
  You have the weaving of!

46

For, as I watch you move, bereft
  Of thought or will or love,
I fear, O listless flames, you weave
The fates of men who strive and grieve.

The web of life, the weft of dreams,
  You weave it ceaselessly;
A strange and filmy thing it seems,
  And made in mystery
Of wind and darkness threaded through
With light these heavens never knew.

O pale, mysterious, wandering fire,
  Born of the earth, alive
With the same breath that I respire,
  Who know and think and strive;
You circle round me, stranger far
Than any charm of any star!

III

Ah me, as faint as you, as slight,
  As hopelessly remote
As you, who still across the night
  Innumerably float,
Intangible as you, I see
The motives of our destiny.

For ah, no angel of the stars,
  No guardian of the soul,
Stoops down beyond the heavenly bars
  Our courses to control.
But filled and nourished with our breath
Are the dim hands that weave our death.

They weave with many threads our souls,
  A subtle-tinted thing,
So interwoven that none controls
  His own imagining,
For every strand with other strands
They twine and bind with viewless hands.

They weave the future of the past;
  Their mystic web is wrought
With dreams from which we woke at last,
  And many a secret thought;
For still they weave, howe'er we strive,
The web new-woven for none alive.

IV

And still the fire-flies come and go—
  Each is a dreamy flame—
Still palely drifting to and fro
  The very way they came—
As though, across the dark they wove
Fate and the shining web thereof.

Yet, even were I sure of it,
  I would not lift a hand
To break the threads that shine and flit—
  For, ah, I understand
Ruin, indeed, I well might leave
But a new web could never weave.

A. Mary F. Robinson.

THE HARE

Through the pale summer grass I stare
  At the blue dome of sky;
A soft, contented, couchant hare
  Hid in the grass am I.

All that I see a hare can see,
  All that I hear she hears,
The wind's wave falling ceaselessly,
  The trembling grassy spears:

The colored patchwork of the weald,
  Unto the world's blue edge,
Green field plaited with yellow field,
  Hedge woven with dark hedge:

And, on the other side, the sea
  Striped by the yellow grass,
Where to and fro continually
  Small busy creatures pass:

Beetles as bright as lustre beads,
  Ladybirds red as blood,
Green grasshoppers like little steeds
  Threading the tangled wood:

And butterflies upon the wind
  Blown past like withered leaves,
Graylings, and all the heathy kind,
  And flecked fritillaries—

Their cool wings flutter near my face
  Where cupped in grass I lie,
Domed with the blue and dazzling space
  Of fine cloud-ruffled sky.

I watch the ambling shadows pass,
  And bask without a care,
With sun and sky and summer grass
  As thoughtless as a hare.

Till from that blue and friendly dome
  There comes a sudden breath,
A shuddering breath out of a tomb,
  A messenger of death.

A sound, a smothering sound, that fills
  And fades, but comes again;
Bruising the gentle grassy hills
  With news of grief and pain.

Oh, then no summer do I see,
  Nor feel the summer air;
But think upon men's cruelty,
  And tremble like a hare.

Sylvia Lynd.

WOUNDS

The wounded bird sped on with shattered wing,
  And gained the holt, and ran a little space,
  Where briar and bracken twined a hiding-place;
There lay and wondered at the grievous thing.

With patient filmy eye he peeped, and heard
  Big blood-drops oozing on the fallen leaf;
  There hour by hour in uncomplaining grief
He watched with pain, but neither cried nor stirred.

The merry sportsmen tramped contented home,
  He heard their happy laughter die away;—
    Across the stubble by the covert-side
    His merry comrades called at eventide;
  They breathed the fragrant air, alert and gay,
And he was sad because his hour was come.

Arthur Christopher Benson.

THE LAMENT OF THE MOLE-CATCHER

An old, sad man who catches moles
   Went lonely down the lane—
All lily-green were the lanes and knolls
   But sorrow numbed his brain.
He paid no heed to flower or weed
   As he went his lonely way.
No note he heard from any bird
   That sang that sad spring day.

"I trapp'd the moles for forty years,
   Who could not see the sky,
I reckoned not blind blood or tears,
   And the Lord has seen them die.
For forty years I've sought to slay
The small, the dumb, the blind,
But now the Lord has made me pay,
   And I am like their kind.
I cannot see or lane or hill,
   Or flower or bird or moon;
Lest life shall lay me lower still,
   O Lord—come take it soon."

Osbert Sitwell.

YESTERNIGHT

Death has come since yesternight,
I met her on the mountainside,
Her face was haggard, drawn and white,
Her robes were ragged and stripped of pride.

I met her near the farthest fold;
I gripped my crook to bar her way,
Then shrank before her eyes' strange cold.
She passed into the twilight grey.

I watched her from the path below
Climb the rugged mountainside
I know not whither, but I know
Someone in the darkness died.

Elfyn Williams David.

THE RETURN

Slow to the precincts of the earthly mind
With many a backward glance returns the soul,
And dimly mourns for what it leaves behind,
And has no pleasure in the distant goal—

Doubtful, as is a rower from the land
When midway on the mere he stays his oar,
And dreams that through the gloom he sees the
    hand
Of one who beckons from the dwindling shore.

E. V. Rieu.

HAPPY WAS I

When the dead man opens his eyes
On bluer rivers and clearer skies,
On brighter flowers in fields more green
Than any the sun he loved has seen . . .

What will he say seeing Beauty there
Fairer than ever and yet less fair
Because the hunger and hope no more
Prey at his heart as they did before?

"Happy was I till the perfect tree
Spread bough and foliage over me
And shook to the grass beside my foot
The lovely, pined-for, ideal fruit.

"Would there were hope of the grave again
Whose mystery baffled the minds of men:
Better the apples my own trees bore . . .
I would that the worm were at the core!"

Edward Davison.

55

THE GHOST

They told her softly I was dead,
  That she should leave me now and rest,
But still she knelt beside the bed,
  Her hair lay heavy on my breast.

I heard her voice against my ear:
  "Not death, not death, but only sleep!"
She did not dream that I could hear,
  Or should be hurt to see her weep.

For I was dead and could not speak,
  For I was dead and could not stir;
Her hand lay up against my cheek,
  And yet I might not comfort her.

So presently she left her dead,
  They soothed her till she ate and slept;
I was a ghost, and on the bed
  There lay the thing for which she wept.

I was a ghost, and had my place
  No more with her humanity;
I looked on what had been my face,
  And thought it wore a smile for me.

But death was dark and very cold,
   And I was lonely and afraid
Without a human hand to hold
   In this new life that death had made.

Till as I stood and shivered there,
   Thrust out from my humanity,
There came a great warm rush of air
   Blowing the darkness back from me:

And there beyond the dark was light,
   And through the light there ran the way:
I left my body in the night,
   My ghost went out into the day.

Vera Larminie.

WINTER DUSK

Dark frost was in the air without,
The dusk was still with cold and gloom,
When less than even a shadow came
    And stood within the room.

But of the three around the fire,
None turned a questioning head to look,
Still read a clear voice, on and on,
    Still stooped they o'er their book.

The children watched their mother's eyes
Moving on softly line to line;
It seemed to listen too—that shade,
    Yet made no outward sign.

The fire-flames crooned a tiny song,
No cold wind moved the wintry tree;
The children both in Faërie dreamed
    Beside their mother's knee.

And nearer yet that spirit drew
Above that heedless one, intent
Only on what the simple words
    Of her small story meant.

No voiceless sorrow grieved her mind,
No memory her bosom stirred,
Nor dreamed she, as she read to two,
    'Twas surely three who heard.

Yet when, the story done, she smiled
From face to face, serene and clear,
A love, half dread, sprang up, as she
    Leaned close and drew them near.

Walter de la Mare.

REVENANTS DES ENFANTS

Softly, on little feet that make no sound,
With laughter that one does not hear, they tread
Upon the primroses that star the ground,
Latticed by shade from branches overhead,
Swaying in moonlight; but their footsteps make
A twinkling like the raindrops on the lake.

The shy things that love silence and the night
Are fearless at their coming; as they pass,
Neither the nightingale nor owl take flight,
So gentle is each footfall on the grass;
They are a part of silence, and a part
Of sweetness sprung from tears hid in the heart.

Their faces we may not caress, nor hear
The little bodies that are soft as dreams;
Their life is rounded by another sphere,
They are as frail as shadows seen in streams:
A ripple might efface them, but they keep
Shadows of their existence in our sleep.

Frederic Manning.

HAUNTED

No sound there is within the little room:
The firelight glows; strange shadows crouch . . .
    and some
Are caught upon the window blind, and come
And go, as folks pass in the outer gloom.
So still it is in here; but in the street
Shrill cries of children; footsteps hurrying past;
Patter of tiny raindrops, thick and fast;
A little gust of wind, sobbing and fleet.
The lamp burns low, no breeze is stirring here,
Time has no place within these dim, still walls
That have known Sorrow, and a living Fear.
I am alone, but there is One who calls:
I am alone, but *She* my vigil keeps,
That Unseen Other One, who weeps . . . and
    weeps.

Molly A. Paley.

GHOST HUNTERS

I thought I heard small voices go
  A-weeping through the night,
And then a pattering of feet
  In panic-stricken flight.

I thought I heard the moonlight rent
  By laughter shrill and cries
That went with echo through the woods
  And crashing down the skies.

But when I leant into the night
  And listened, still and tense
There was no panic in the air
  Nor any turbulence.

A silence lay on field and wood;
  A silence, breathing deep.
Beneath a canopy of stars
  The world was fast asleep.

Violet Le Maistre.

FAERIE

Under the edge of midnight
  While my love is far away,
A wind from the world of faerie
  Blows between day and day.

And wandering thoughts possess me,
  Such as no wise man knows,
Death and a thousand accidents,
  And high impossible woes.

Whether now in her pastime
  She turned a little, sighed
With the heaviness of breathing,
  And even in turning died:

Or whether some cloud covers
  The lobes of the conscious brain
And all that she knew aforetime
  She shall never know again,

But her friends shall bring her to me,
  Bewildered and afraid
Lest a stranger's hand should touch her,
  A shrinking alien maid,—

Yet such distress in patience
  And faith an end may find,
And a more fantastic peril
  Moves in my dreaming mind:

None knows how deep within us
  Lies hid a secret flaw,
Where spins the mad world ever
  On the very edge of law.

Under the chance that rules us
  Anarchic terrors stir,
Lest what to me has happened
  Has never happened to her.

First love in our first meeting,
  Changed eyes, and bridal vows,
The incredible years together
  Lived in a single house,

The kisses born of custom
  That are sweeter and stranger still
Than any clasp of passion,
  And the shaping of one will,—

Was it some wraith deceived me,
  And lives she still apart
In her father's house contented,
  With an unawakened heart?

Now at this striking midnight
  Through the chink between day and day,

Has a wind from the world of faerie
  Blown all my life away?

Here am I now left naked
  Of the vapour that was she:
While the true maid 'midst her kindred
  Has never thought of me?

For ten long years together
  Can a thing be and not be,
Till it ceases to be for ever,—
  And has this chanced to me?

Charles Williams.

SHE WHOM I LOVE WILL SIT APART

She whom I love will sit apart,
  And they whom love makes wise
May know the beauty in her heart
  By the beauty in her eyes.

Thoughts that in quietness confute
  The noisy world are hers,
Like music in a listening lute
  Whose strings no finger stirs.

And in her eyes the shadows move,
  Not glad nor sad, but strange
With those unchanging dreams that prove
  The littleness of change.

Gerald Gould.

ABSENT AND PRESENT

Through morning meads we broke the dew,
  And heard the hidden skylark sing,
Oh, goodly sound, when, having you,
  I wanted for no other thing!
And ah, how plainly cried his tongue—
"All grief is old, all joy is young!"

Through moving mists around the wood
  The daylight came in grey disguise,
A pallid ghost. Then as we stood,
  I marked the hunger of your eyes;
And all your thoughts had flown away,
Back to the East and far Cathay!

For ever in your veins must run
  The rover's blood, so strange to me!
You heard the call; you saw the sun
  Rise red across the Indian sea;
So sundered stood we, side by side—
Two fates which seas and lands divide!

And now alone through twilit mead,
  I break the dew: yet not alone,

Still, as the skylark sings, I read
   As fair a meaning in its tone;
For now he sings of you, my dear,
"The near is far, the far is near!"

Laurence Housman.

THE NIGHT WIND

The night wind taps on my window,
  But you knocked on my heart's closed door.
    I shall always know
    When the soft winds blow,
  And my clipped wings are trying to soar—
That out of the cool night shadows
  You knocked on my heart's closed door.

The moonlight falls through my window,
  And it silvers my chamber floor;
    When its drifting thread
    Creeps under my bed,
  Then I see you again as of yore—
You stood in the throbbing stillness
  And knocked at my heart's closed door.

The darkness beats on my window
  And it leans on my heart's closed door;
    When its wings I hear,
    I shall always fear
  That you came: but return nevermore—
Pass on through the dusky silence
  That curtains my heart's closed door.
    You pass on your way,
    Deaf when I say—
  "Wait! I have opened the door."

                              Edith M. Walker.

69

LOGIE KIRK

O Logie Kirk amang the braes,
  I'm thinking o' the merry days
Afore I trod thae weary ways
  That led me far frae Logie!

Fine do I mind when I was young
  Abune thy graves the mavis sung
An' ilka birdie had a tongue
  To ca' me back to Logie.

O Logie Kirk, tho' aye the same
  The burn sings ae remembered name,
There's ne'er a voice to cry "Come hame
  To bonnie Bess at Logie!"

Far, far awa' the years decline
  That took the lassie wha was mine
An' laid her sleepin' lang, lang syne
  Amang the braes at Logie.

                    Violet Jacob.

DUNSFORT BOG

To Cahirmone I walked one day
  Away across the glen
To where the busy stonechats nest
  And foxes make their den.

The plovers wheeled above my head
  As I went whistling by,
And merry larks with hovering wings
  Rose up against the sky.

And loud I whistled as I went
  Along the heathered hill,
Until I came to Cahirmone;
  Then sudden I stood still.

For there, the lovelight in her face,
  I saw my lover stand,
But ah! 'twas not myself she saw,
  Nor me she clasped by hand.

Then quickly hushed the bunting's song,
  While dark clouds filled the sky,
And dropped their tears upon the stones
  That strewed the ground near by.

And back I turned from Cahirmone
   Away across the glen
By Dunsfort Bog where, it is said,
   Lie many long-dead men.

And wet and cold the mist that blew,
   And sad the curlew's cry,
As I passed by the still, black pools
   Where wild things go to die.

Miriam A. Coppinger.

THE WATERMILL

I'll rise at midnight and I'll rove
Up the hill and down the drove
   That leads to the old unnoticed mill,
And think of one I used to love:
There stooping to the hunching wall
   I'll stare into the rush of stars
Or bubbles that the waterfall
   Brings forth and breaks in ceaseless wars.

The shelving hills have made a form
Where the mill holdings shelter warm,
   And here I came with one I loved
To watch the seething millions swarm.
But long ago she grew a ghost
   Through walking with me every day;
Even when her beauty burned me most
   She to a spectre dimmed away—

Until though cheeks all morning-bright
And black eyes gleaming life's delight
   And singing voice dwelt in my sense,
Herself paled on my inward sight.
She grew one whom deep waters glassed.
   Then in dismay I hid from her,

And lone by talking brooks at last
  I found a Love still lovelier.

O lost in tortured days of France!
Yet still the moment comes like chance
  Born in the stirring midnight's sigh
Or in the wild wet sunset's glance:
And how I know not but this stream
  Still sounds like vision's voice, and still
I watch with Love the bubbles gleam,
  I walk with Love beside the mill.

The heavens are thralled with cloud, yet gray,
Half-moonlight swims the field till day,
  The stubbled fields, the bleaching woods;—
Even this bleak hour was stolen away.
By this shy water falling low
  And calling low the whole night through
And calling back the long ago
  And richest world I ever knew.

The hop-kiln fingers cobweb-white
With discord dim turned left and right,
  And when the wind was south and small
The sea's far whisper drowsed the night;
Scarce more than mantling ivy's voice
  That in the tumbling water trailed.
Love's spirit called me to rejoice
  When she to nothingness had paled.

For Love the daffodils shone here
In grass the greenest of the year,
  Daffodils seemed the sunset lights

And silver birches budded clear:
And all from east to west there strode
  Great shafted clouds in argent air,
The shining chariot-wheels of God,
  And still Love's moment sees them there.

Edmund Blunden.

THE WEATHER-VANE

O Steeple-Cock, stoop down to me
   And tell me what you see afar!
A sail that flickers on the sea
   No bigger than a star.

O make your fledge a beacon, fowl,
   And let your wings be lanterns both!
Afar I see the tempest scowl
   And all the waves are wroth.

Look well again, good steeple-cock,
   And can you see her lantern-spark?
Nay, now she runs upon a rock,
   And founders in the dark.

O steeple-cock, say one is saved,
   One only lad, that shall not drown!
I saw a sudden hand that waved
   But once, and then went down.

Fly, steeple-cock, with my true pledge,
   And say I love him, ere he die!
Too heavy is my golden fledge,
   Good lass! *I cannot fly.*

Wilfrid Thorley.

THE DREAMER

Tread softly by, shapes of remembered care,
Nor stir night's gentle fingers from her eyes.
She sleeps, and open to the vaulted skies
The Earth sleeps with her: land and ocean share
One dream; and on the darkened roads of air
Her spirit mounts, where timid rays and few
Steal down between the late and early dew
From starry lamps by many a windy stair.

She moves in music through a lustrous land
That needs no moon by night nor any star,
Moves where the sources of the morning are,
And doors that open to the dreamer's hand,
And greetings dear as on the desert sand
The voice of running waters. Wake her not:
Those melodies, scarce heard, are soon forgot,
And all the long-drawn leagues too swiftly spanned.

E. V. Rieu.

HAUNTED

Dear Eyes that smile to me across the years
How we have drifted, drifted! since the day
When through an arrowy rain of April tears
I met you down the arching woodland way!
Under the swaying, wet wild-apple boughs
You leaned and lingered, white as petals blown,
And heart to heart, between our passionate vows
      I held you, all my own!

Now I am old and tired, and Love's strong flame
That lit our lives to ecstasy divine
Burns faint and low; yet, speaking soft your name
When twilight falls, I still can call you mine!
For, dim against the dying firelight's glow,
A gentle wraith, through mists of Memory
As through the arrowy rain of long ago
      You come again to me!

Esther Raworth.

THE SHADOW

She loitered on the high road, she hastened in the
    lane,
At every turn before her the shadow turned again.

She lingered in the valley, she climbed across the
    hill,
But all the way beside her the shadow flitted still.

She came into the homestead, she entered by the
    door,
But close against the lintel the shadow went before.

She stayed beside the hearthstone, she took the
    wonted place,
But from the faces round her the shadow hid her
    face.

She lay beneath the yew trees, the earth upon her
    breast,
But on the grass above her the shadow lay at rest.

Vera Larminie.

THE RE-BIRTH OF THE SOUL

(Written on the recent death of my aged mother in Spring)

Now what have I to do with Death?
And what has Death to do with me?
The winds are sweet with vernal breath.
The birds are singing in the tree.

And yet she droops her hands—and dies,
My mother who ordained my birth;
And 'tis the mating-time of earth,
Of linnet-song and cuckoo cries;

When every wing is in the air,
And every seedling seeks to rise:
And plants uplift their banners fair
Before my sad unsleeping eyes.

Ah! Winter claims her for his own,
For very tired and old she lies.
Outside no wrecking north winds moan,
Only within Life's Autumn dies.

Take comfort! Spring is even here;
It struggles from this husk of pain.
Time turns the seed-rind dull and sere
That youth may leap to life again.

Herbert E. Palmer.

IN SPRING

Wistful in loveliness beyond all words
Are April woods when spring has crowned the hills;
Heart-ache it is to hear the song of birds
At twilight in the time of daffodils.

In the bright orchard when the wind was sweet
I stood beneath the pear-tree mossed with green,
A shower of blossoms drifting to my feet—
Never such shining wonder have I seen!

Oh! beautiful the days beyond all words,
Gentle the nights, when Spring has crossed the hills!
Why then these tears to hear the song of birds
At twilight in the time of daffodils?

Molly Young.

ARCADY IN ENGLAND

I met some children in a wood,
A happy and tumultuous rout
That came with many a wanton shout
And darted hither and about
(As in a stream the fickle trout),
To ease their pagan lustihood.

And in their midst they led along
A goat with wreaths about his neck
That they had taken pains to deck
To join that bacchanalian throng.

And one of them was garlanded
With strands of wild convolvulus
About his ringlets riotous,
And carried rowan-berries red.

And one, the eldest of the band,
Whose life was seven summers glad,
Was all in flowered muslin clad,
And naked dancing feet she had
To lead the sylvan saraband.
With hazel skin and coral bead
A gipsy dryad of the mead

She seemed; she led the gay stampede
With fruited branches in her hand.

For all were bearing autumn fruit;
Some, apples on the loaded bough,
And pears that on the orchard's brow
With damask-plums were hanging now;
And much they had of woodland loot,
Of berries black and berries blue,
Of fir-cones, and of medlars too;
And one, who bore no plunder, blew
On reeds like an Arcadian flute.

They passed, and still I stood knee-deep
In thymy grass to watch their train.
They wound along the wooded lane
And crossed a streamlet with a leap,
And as I saw them once again
They passed a shepherd and his sheep.

And you might think, I made this song
For joy of song as I strode along
One day between the Kentish shaws,
Slashing at scarlet hips and haws.
But thinking so, you nothing know
Of children taken unawares,
Of tinkers' tents among the gorse,
The poor lean goat, the hobbled horse,
And painted vans for country fairs.

V. Sackville-West.

FINE EVENING

To-night the sky is like a rose
 Above the little town,
A petal fallen from a rose
 The chalk-pit on the down.

The ancient vane is gilt again,
 And every roof is warm,
And brightly burns a window-pane
 In some far distant farm.

The gentle hill, the gentle sky
 Lie close as close-shut lips,
Softly and very secretly
 Day towards darkness slips.

And every tree its arms puts out
 To clasp the passing light,
And every bud puts up its mouth
 To kiss the day good-night—

The elm-trees all on tip-toe stand
 Day's going to behold,
Like little children hand-in-hand
 With hair of misty gold—

So slowly that she seems to stay,
    So slowly does she pass!
But trace we may the steps of day
    Translucent in the grass.

To-night her going is as kind
    As if that she stood still,
And we, by climbing, noon should find,
    Full noon, behind the hill.

Sylvia Lynd.

THE LANE

There is a little lane that lies
    Far from the haunts of men;
And O! the heart within me cries
    To tread its ways again.

Low is its voice and very sweet,
    —The young wind whispering,
The lilt of song where waters meet,
    The call of birds in Spring.

Soft are its hands and very kind
    Outstretched to welcome me,
—Pale honeysuckle boughs entwined
    With heart-leaved bryony.

Bright are its eyes and very clear;
    Starred in the wayside grass
The golden-hearted daisies peer
    All smiling as I pass.

Pure is its heart and very wise,
    Far from the haunts of men;
And O! the heart within me cries
    To hear it beat again.

H. Ross.

REMEMBRANCE

O places I have seen upon the earth,
  Your silence is not virginal any more,
For one still wanders there whose mortal birth
  Was mine. And now, gaze bent on buried lore,

A child, a youth, a man—O is it I?—
  In silence stands by every lake and tree,
Or leans lost poring face where flickering by
  The bright stream moves on to another sea.

And all is changed, the shining fields, the host
  Of shapes who were myself years long ago.
'Tis these who love! And I am but a ghost
  Exiled from their sole light and jealous glow.

Ah no, it was not I who, laughing there,
  Walked with the crowd, and there, in solitude,
Wandered a summer's day through windless air,
  In a once-visited far-northern wood.

It was not I from morn till noon who went
  The white road's length to the white noisy town
So many years ago. That light is spent,
  And he who saw it, long since fallen down.

And he no less, the child who, walking grave,
    Saw beauty of tiny weed, of moss and stone;
And all his comrades, diffident and brave—
    They each have perished, silent and alone.

I can no more have speech with them, nor know
    The light which lights them. Vaster than the sea,
The yawning distances o'er which we go
    On our frail paths of sundering destiny.

Edwin Muir.

THE RETURN

All day the land in golden sunshine lay,
All day a happy people to and fro
Moved through the quiet summer fields; all day
I wandered with bowed head and footstep slow,
A stranger in the well-remembered place,
Where Time has left not one familiar face
I knew long years ago.

By marsh lands golden with bog asphodel,
I saw the fitful plover wheel and scream;
The soft winds swayed the foxglove's purple bell;
The iris trembled by the whispering stream;
Gazing on those blue hills which know not change,
All the dead years seemed fallen dim and strange
Unreal as a dream.

Unchanged as in my dreams lay the fair land,—
The laughter-loving lips, the eager feet,
The hands that struck warm welcome to my hand,
The hearts that at my coming higher beat,
Have long been cold in death; no glad surprise
Wakens for me in any living eyes,
That once made life so sweet.

Slowly the day drew down the golden west;
The purple shadows lengthened on the plain,
Yet I unresting through a world at rest,
Went silent with my memory and my pain;
Then for a little space, across the years
To me, bowed down with time and worn with tears,
My friends came back again.

By many a spot where summer could not last,
In other days for all our joy too long,
They came about me from the shadowy past,
As last I saw them, young and gay and strong;
And she, my heart, came fair as in the days
When at her coming all the radiant ways
Thrilled into happy song.

Ah me! ah me! on such a summer night
In silence here together, she and I
Stood watching the pale, lingering fringe of light
Go slowly creeping round the northern sky.
Ah, love, if all the weary years could give
But one sweet hour of that sweet night to live
With thee—and then to die!

The old sweet fragrance fills the summer air,
The same light lingers on the northern sea,
Still, as of old, the silent land lies fair
Beneath the silent stars, the melody
Of moving waters still is on the shore,
And I am here again—but nevermore
Will she come back to me.

Duncan J. Robertson.

GOD'S HILLS

In our hill country of the North
  The rainy skies are soft and grey,
And rank on rank the clouds go forth,
  And rain in orderly array
Treads the mysterious flanks of hills
  That stood before our race began,
And still shall stand when Sorrow spills
  Her last tear on the dust of man.

There shall the mists in beauty break,
  And clinging tendrils finely drawn
A rose and silver glory make
  About the silent feet of dawn;
Till Gable clears his iron sides
  And Bowfell's wrinkled front appears,
And Scawfell's clustered might derides
  The menace of the marching years.

The tall men of that noble land
  Who share such high companionship,
Are scorners of the feeble hand,
  Contemners of the faltering lip.
When all the ancient truths depart
  In every strait that men confess,

91

Stands in the stubborn Cumbrian heart
  The spirit of that steadfastness.

In quiet valleys of the hills
  The humble grey stone crosses lie,
And all day long the curlew shrills,
  And all day long the wind goes by.
But on some stifling alien plain
  The flesh of Cumbrian men is thrust
In shallow pits, and cries in vain
  To mingle with its kindred dust.

Yet those make death a little thing
  Who know the settled works of God,
Winds that heard Latin watchwords ring
  From ramparts where the Romans trod,
Stars that beheld the last King's crown
  Flash in the steel grey mountain tarn,
And ghylls that cut the live rock down
  Before kings ruled in Ispahan.

And when the sun at even dips
  And Sabbath bells are sad and sweet,
When some wan Cumbrian mother's lips
  Pray for the son they shall not greet;
As falls that sudden dew of grace
  Which makes for her the riddle plain,
The South wind blows to our own place,
  And we shall see the hills again.

William Noel Hodgson.

THE WILD GEESE

"O tell me what was on yer road, ye roarin' norlan'
    Wind,
As ye cam blawin' frae the land that's niver frae my
    mind?
My feet they traivel England, but I'm dee'in for
    the north."
"My man, I heard the siller tides rin up the Firth
    o' Forth."

"Aye, Wind, I ken them weel eneuch, and fine they
    fa' an' rise,
And fain I'd feel the creepin' mist on yonder shore
    that lies,
But tell me, ere ye passed them by, what saw ye on
    the way?"
"My man, I rocked the rovin' gulls that sail abune
    the Tay."

"But saw ye naething, leein' Wind, afore ye cam'
    to Fife?
There's muckle lyin' 'yont the Tay that's mair to
    me nor life."

"My man, I swept the Angus braes ye hae'na trod
    for years."
"O Wind, forgi'e a hameless loon that canna see for
    tears!"

"And far abune the Angus straths I saw the wild
    geese flee,
A lang, lang skein o' beatin' wings, wi' their heids
    towards the sea,
And aye their cryin' voices trailed ahint them on
    the air—"
"O Wind, hae maircy, haud yer whisht, for I daurna
    listen mair!"

Violet Jacob.

THE QUIET HOUSE

'Tis very quiet in the house
  Without the turbulent little flock.
The sweet hours, quiet as a mouse,
  Steal slowly round the ticking clock.
We gather honey while we may
When children are at school all day.

So peaceful with the song of birds,
  The water lapping on the shore;
But evening brings the flocks and herds
  And happy children home once more.
Blessed the hour in sun or rain
That brings the children home again.

'Tis very quiet in the house
  Where children come not home at all.
The day goes stiller than a mouse;
  Gulls and the sea-winds cry and call:
And two old shadows by the flame
Talk of the days when children came.

Oh, when the children are away,
  The house is very still and sweet.
But if no evening, gold or gray,
  Brought the quick kiss, the flying feet,
Heavily would the silence press,
The loneliness, the loneliness!

Katherine Tynan.

LONELINESS

When graven is the tale of man's distress
Above the tomb of all our humankind,
Let there be told the torment of the mind
Of him who knows the spirit's loneliness.
Death ever changing, changeless comes to all,
And love brings joy, all strangely wrought with pain,
That he who greatly dares may greatly gain;
But loneliness, whose cold imperious call
Rings through the world to bid his chosen come,
Stands jealous as some pagan god of old,
Demanding sacrifice of grief and tears.
Who hears his summons evermore is dumb,
Who knows him lord, mates agony untold
And trails a chain of bondage through the years.

N. J. Kessler.

IN SEPTEMBER

Still are the meadowlands, and still
Ripens the upland corn,
And over the brown gradual hill
The moon has dipped a horn.

The voices of the dear unknown
With silent hearts now call,
My rose of youth is overblown
And trembles to the fall.

My song forsakes me like the birds
That leave the rain and grey,
I hear the music of the words
My lute can never say.

Francis Ledwidge.

TUMULT

Through the storm and the desolate night there was
      far away heard
  The cry of a plover that wailed like a soul with-
      out sight;
And a horror of darkness enveloped the land and
      bestirred
  Through the storm and the desolate night.

As the wind in the trees goeth wistfully forth to the
      dark,
  Like a querulous voice ineffectually pleading for
      ease
Must the Spirit be poured into sound to which no
      one will hark—
  As the wind in the trees?

As the call of a bird in the night is the voice that is
      I;—
  And hasten, O Dawn, and illumine me, Send me
      thy light,
Lest I pass as a gust in the trees, lest I utterly die
  As the call of a bird in the night.

C. B. Tracey.

THE DARK WAY

Rougher than death the road I choose
Yet shall my feet not walk astray,
Though dark, my way I shall not lose
For this way is the darkest way.

Set but a limit to the loss
And something shall at last abide,
The blood-stained beams that formed the cross,
The thorns that crowned the crucified;

But who shall lose all things in One,
Shut out from Heaven and the Pit
Shall lose the darkness and the sun,
The finite and the infinite;

And who shall see in one small flower
The chariots and the thrones of might
Shall be in peril from that hour
Of blindness and the endless night;

And who shall hear in one short name
Apocalyptic thunders seven
His heart shall flicker like a flame
'Twixt Hell's gates and the gates of Heaven.

For I have seen your body's grace,
The miracle of the flowering rod,
And in the beauty of your face
The glory of the face of God,

And I have heard the thunderous roll
Clamored from heights of prophecy,
Your splendid name, and from my soul
Uprose the clouds of minstrelsy.

Now I have chosen in the dark
The desolate way to walk alone
Yet strive to keep alive one spark
Of your known grace and grace unknown;

And when I leave you lest my love
Should seal your spirit's ark with clay
Spread your bright wings, O shining Dove—
But my way is the darkest way.

Joseph Mary Plunkett.

PERSONALITY

As one who goes between high garden walls,
Along a road that never has an end,
With still the empty way behind, in front,
Which he must pace for evermore alone—
So, even so, is Life to every soul,
Walled in with barriers that no Love can break.

And yet! ah me! how often would we break
Through every fence, and overleap the walls,
And link ourselves to some beloved soul,
Hearing her answering voice until the end,
Going her chosen way, no more alone,
But happy comrades, seeing Heaven in front.

But, ah, the barrier's high! and still my front
I dash against the stones in vain, nor break
A passage through, but still remain alone:
Hearing sometimes across the garden walls
A voice the wind brings over, or an end
Of song that sinks like dew into my soul.

Since others sing, let me forget, my Soul,
How dreary-long the road goes on in front,
And tow'rds how flat, inevitable an end.
Come, let me look for daisies, let me break
The gillyflowers that shelter in the walls—
But ah! it is so sad to be alone!

For ever, irremediably alone,
Not only I or thou, but every soul,
Each cased and fastened with invisible walls.
Shall we go mad with it? or bear a front
Of desperate courage doomed to fail and break?
Or trudge in sullen patience till the end?

Ah, hope of every heart, there is an end!
An end when each shall be no more alone,
But either dead, or strong enough to break
This prisoning self and find that larger Soul
(Neither of thee nor me) enthroned in front
Of Time, beyond the world's remotest walls!

I trust the end and sing within my walls,
Sing all alone, to bid some listening soul
Wait till the day break, watch for me in front!

                    A. Mary F. Robinson.

SURSUM COR!

Lament no more, my heart, lament no more,
Though all these clouds have covered up the light,
And thou, so far from shore,
Art baffled in mid flight;
Still proudly as in joy through sorrow soar!
As the wild swan,
Voyaging over dark and rising seas,
Into the stormy air adventures on
With wide unfaltering wings, the way he bore
When blue the water laughed beneath the breeze
And morning round the radiant beaches shone.
So thou through all this pain
Endure, my heart, whither thy course was bound;
Though never may the longed-for goal be found,
Thy steadfast will maintain.
Thou must not fail, for nothing yet hath failed
Which was to thee most dear and most adored;
Still glorious is Love, thy only lord,
Truth still is true, and sweetness still is sweet:
The high stars have not changed, nor the sun paled.
Still warmly, O my heart, and bravely beat.
Remember not how lovely was delight,
How piteous is pain,
Keep, keep thy passionate flight,
Nor find thy voyage vain,
Yea, till thou break, my heart, all meaner quest
    disdain.

Laurence Binyon.

103

EVENING

When little lights in little ports come out,
Quivering down through water with the stars,
And all the fishing fleet of slender spars
Range at their moorings, veer with tide about;

When race of wind is stilled, and sails are furled,
And underneath our single riding-light
The curve of black-ribbed deck gleams palely white,
And slumbrous waters pool a slumbrous world,

—Then, and then only, have I thought how sweet
Old age might sink upon a windy youth,
Quiet beneath the riding-light of truth,
Weathered through storms, and gracious in retreat.

V. Sackville-West.

ON GROWING OLD

Be with me, Beauty, for the fire is dying;
My dog and I are old, too old for roving.
Man, whose young passion sets the spindrift flying,
Is soon too lame to march, too cold for loving.
I take the book and gather to the fire,
Turning old yellow leaves; minute by minute
The clock ticks to my heart. A withered wire,
Moves a thin ghost of music in the spinet.
I cannot sail your seas, I cannot wander
Your cornland, nor your hill-land, nor your valleys
Ever again, nor share the battle yonder
Where the young knight the broken squadron rallies.
Only stay quiet while my mind remembers
The beauty of fire from the beauty of embers.

Beauty, have pity! for the strong have power,
The rich their wealth, the beautiful their grace,
Summer of man its sunlight and its flower,
Spring-time of man all April in a face.
Only, as in the jostling in the Strand,
Where the mob thrusts or loiters or is loud,
The beggar with the saucer in his hand
Asks only a penny from the passing crowd,
So, from this glittering world with all its fashion,

Its fire, and play of men, its stir, its march,
Let me have wisdom, Beauty, wisdom and passion,
Bread to the soul, rain where the summers parch.
Give me but these, and, though the darkness close,
Even the night will blossom as the rose.

John Masefield.

THE LAST MEMORY

When I am old, and think of the old days,
And warm my hands before a little blaze,
Having forgotten love, hope, fear, desire,
I shall see, smiling out of the pale fire.
One face, mysterious and exquisite;
And I shall gaze and ponder over it,
Wondering, was it Leonardo wrought
That stealthy ardency, where passionate thought
Burns inward, a revealing flame, and glows
To the last ecstasy, which is repose?
Was it Bronzino, those Borghese eyes?
And, musing thus among my memories,
O unforgotten! you will come to seem,
As pictures do, remembered, some old dream.
And I shall think of you as something strange
And beautiful, and full of helpless change,
Which I beheld and carried in my heart;
But you I loved will have become a part
Of the eternal mystery, and love
Like a dim pain; and I shall bend above
My little fire, and shiver, being cold,
When you are no more young, and I am old.

Arthur Symons.

THE OLD WOMAN

Oh! I am old, and sad, and sleepy-eyed,
But I have known the dreams none ever knew.
The stars have kissed my face, the dews my feet;
But now the shadows come into my eyes,
And I have half forgotten fairy ways.

But I will go and sit and dream of them,
And dream of all the fairies on the hill;
Until I see them dancing on the grass;
Until I hear them laughing with the wind,
And singing to me of a place apart
Where cold white water gleams beneath pale skies,
And mystic fir trees stand upon the hill.

I hear the light wind murmur in the grass;
And in the trees I see strange gleaming lights.
I hear a murmur in the rising wind—

"Oh! you are old, three times too old for us;
But we will make you young and fair of face.
Oh! fair and pale is water at the dawn,
But fairest are the people of the hill.

"Oh! you are going, going; you are gone
To where the fairies dance upon the hill.

Then you will dance with us in lonely woods,
And you will sing beside the silent lake
Until the wind has lost its song; until
The mountains fall, and this old world is dead.
Come with us, old, old woman, come away.
Oh! sad, and grey, and sleepy-headed—come!"

Marjorie Holmes.

THE COUNSEL OF GILGAMESH

"Gilgamesh, why dost thou wander around?
Life, which thou seekest, thou canst not find."

Epic of Gilgamesh.

Why wander round, Gilgamesh?
  The sun that set to-night
Shall climb the sky to-morrow
  And bake the world with light.
Throughout the undying ages
  The sun shall set and rise
As it hath set and risen
  From dim eternities.

Why wander round, Gilgamesh?
  Why vainly wander round?
What canst thou find, O seeker,
  Which hath not long been found?
What canst thou know, O scholar,
  Which hath not long been known?
What canst thou have, O spoiler,
  Which dead men did not own?

The camel of the desert,
  The wild ape of the wood,

Tread the white bones of heroes
　Who in thy place once stood;
Like thee, they felt the sunshine,
　Like thee, they loved the day,
Like thee, they sought and suffered—
　And thou shalt be as they.

And other men, Gilgamesh,
　Shall seek what thou dost seek,
And to their youth and ardour
　Thy rotting bones shall speak.
They will not heed thy counsel,
　They too will wander round,
And waste their years in seeking
　That which hath long been found.

Why wander round, Gilgamesh?
　Why vainly wander round?
What canst thou find, O seeker,
　Which hath not long been found?
What canst thou know, O scholar,
　Which dead men did not know?

And this was asked in Nineveh
　Thousands of years ago.

Sheila Kaye-Smith.

A THOUGHT IN TWO MOODS

I saw it—pink and white—revealed
  Upon the white and green;
The white and green was a daisied field,
  The pink and white Ethleen.

And as I looked it seemed in kind
  That difference they had none;
The two fair bodiments combined
  As varied miens of one.

A sense that, in some mouldering year,
  As one they both would lie,
Made me move quickly on to her
  To pass the pale thought by.

She laughed and said: "Out there, to me,
  You looked so weather-browned,
And brown in clothes, you seemed to be
  Made of the dusty ground!"

Thomas Hardy.

DISILLUSION

I stood in Heaven at last and gravely scanned
Sad angel hosts, their fabled glory sped;
One placed a halo round my warrior head,
And cast beneath his feet the shining brand
Wherewith this arm had striven to purge a land
Sin-sick and vile, and sorrow-visited.
And now, alas! another in my stead
Shall build the radiant city I had planned,
And win the high renown for which I fought!
I for eternity must lie and drowse
In halcyon fields, my soul ignobly sure,
Crowned with a misted circlet angel-wrought . . .
For *him* the tilt, the fight, the great carouse,
While I the turgid peace of Heaven endure.

Winifred N. James.

LOVE OF LIFE

I cannot leave the splendor of the sky
Or the dear whispers of the summer grass,
The little, secret shadow of wings that pass
Above moon-daisies, or the wistful sigh
Of woods at dusk. Oh! Heaven is all too high
When on the earth the infinite colors start
And honeysuckle rushes to my heart . . .
Leave me my human pain: I cannot die!

Beauty and Love in little moonlit ways
Of silence; June, when roses flash to birth;
Youth and the love-time of the summer days . . .
Oh! Heaven is cold and Death comes all too soon.
I cannot die when roses laugh in June.
And You—and You—are lovely on the earth.

C. A. Renshaw.

OUT OF WEAKNESS

To-day, as far as eye can see,
　　Or thought can multiply the sight,
In tangled croft, on upland lea,
　　A message flashed along the light
Has worked strange marvels underground,
　　And stirred a million sleeping cells,
The rose has hopes of being crowned;
　　The foxglove dreams of purple bells;

No tiny life that blindly strives,
　　But thinks the impulse all his own,
Nor dreams that countless other lives
　　Like him are groping, each alone;
What dizzy sweetness, when the rain
　　Has wept her fill of laden showers,
To peep across the teeming plain,
　　Through miles of upward-springing flowers!

The brown seed bursts his armoured cap,
　　And slips a white-veined arm between;
White juicy stalks, a touch would snap,
　　And twisted horns of sleekest green
Now shift and turn from side to side,
　　And fevered drink the stealing rain,

As children fret at sermon-tide,
  When roses kiss the leaded pane.

The tender, the resistless grace,
  That stirs the hopes of sleeping flowers,
Could shake yon fortress to her base,
  And splinter those imperial towers;
Concentred, bound, obedient,
  The soul that lifts those dreaming lids
Could mock old Ram'ses' monument,
  And pile a thousand pyramids.

Arthur Christopher Benson.

HORSES

Those lumbering horses in the steady plough,
On the bare field—I wonder why, just now,
They seemed so terrible, so wild and strange,
Like magic power on the stony grange.

Perhaps some childish hour has come again,
When I watched fearful, through the blackening
    rain,
Their hooves like pistons in an ancient mill
Move up and down, yet seem as standing still.

Their conquering hooves which trod the stubble
    down
Were ritual which turned the field to brown,
And their great hulks were seraphim of gold,
Or mute ecstatic monsters on the mould.

And oh the rapture when, one furrow done,
They marched broad-breasted to the sinking sun!
The light flowed off their bossy sides in flakes;
The furrows rolled behind like struggling snakes.

But when at dusk with steaming nostrils home
They came, they seemed gigantic in the gloam,

And warm and glowing with mysterious fire,
Which lit their smouldering bodies in the mire.

Their eyes as brilliant and as wide as night
Gleamed with a cruel apocalyptic sight.
Their manes the leaping ire of the wind
Lifted with rage invisible and blind.

Ah now it fades! it fades! and I must pine
Again for that dread country crystalline,
Where the blank field and the still-standing tree
Were bright and fearful presences to me.

Edwin Muir.

THE SEED SHOP

Here in a quiet and dusty room they lie,
Faded as crumbled stone or shifting sand,
Forlorn as ashes, shrivelled, scentless, dry—
Meadows and gardens running through my hand.

Dead that shall quicken at the call of Spring,
Sleepers to stir beneath June's magic kiss,
Though birds pass over, unremembering,
And no bee seeks here roses that were his.

In this brown husk a dale of hawthorn dreams,
A cedar in this narrow cell is thrust
That will drink deeply of a century's streams,
These lilies shall make summer on my dust.

Here in their safe and simple house of death,
Sealed in their shells a million roses leap;
Here I can blow a garden with my breath,
And in my hand a forest lies asleep.

Muriel Stuart.

THE GIANT PUFFBALL

From what sad star I know not, but I found
   Myself new-born below the coppice rail,
No bigger than the dewdrops and as round,
   In a soft sward no cattle might assail.

And so I gathered mightiness and grew
   With this one dream kindling in me, that I
Should never cease from conquering light and dew
   Till my white splendor touched the trembling
      sky.

A century of blue and stilly light
   Bowed down before me, the dew came again,
The moon my sibyl worshipped through the night,
   The sun returned and long abode; but then

Hoarse drooping darkness hung me with a shroud
   And switched at me with shrivelled leaves in
      scorn.
Red morning stole beneath a grinning cloud,
   And suddenly clambering over dyke and thorn

A half-moon host of churls with flags and sticks
   Hallooed and hurtled up the partridge brood,

And Death clapped hands from all the echoing
    thicks,
  And trampling envy spied me where I stood;

Who haled me tired and quaking, hid me by,
  And came again after an age of cold,
And hung me in the prison-house adry
  From the great crossbeam. Here defiled and cold

I perish through unnumbered hours, I swoon,
  Hacked with harsh knives to staunch a child's
    torn hand;
And all my hopes must with my body soon
  Be but as crouching dust and wind-blown sand.

                    Edmund Blunden.

THE SOULS IN PRISON

I passed beyond the barrier of the tomb
    Into a cheerless land
Where all was dead, as when the winter gloom
    Touches with icy hand
The verdure of the earth's congealing womb
    And makes the rivers stand.

It was a realm of banishèd delight;
    (Nor nightingale nor lark
To hail the day or close the eye of night—)
    A silence grim and stark,
As when eclipse hides sun or moon from sight
    And all the land is dark.

A lurid twilight, as when sullen ground
    Or apprehensive tree
Waits till the rumble of the thunder sound
    Foretells a wrath to be.
So loomed the heavy stillness, and around
    Stretched a black, angry sea.

Nor sight nor sound was on that tideless shore,
    Nor any that made moan,
And where I would, I wandered evermore
    (My will was all mine own).

And never, never had I felt before
  So utterly alone.

And then the agony of a silent voice
  Beat throbbing on my brain,
"Lo! I am with thee, comrade of thy choice,
  For happiness or pain:
Rejoice with me!" And at the word "Rejoice!"
  The blood froze in each vein.

"Here is thy portion, where a place is given
  For thee and me to dwell.—
And I am of thy making: hast thou striven
  To mould me ill or well?
For in Remembrance wilt thou find thy Heaven
  Or thine abiding Hell.

"Remove the threads that hold my veil in place
  (Threads from the web, Despair).
O, fellow prisoner, look upon my face
  And tell me I am fair.
I am the spirit of forgotten days,
  Ghost of the things that were.

"Come, from my brow the covering withdraw,
  And claim me here for thine."—
The throbbing ceased: the veil I loosed in awe
  That face to unconfine.
It fell—I shrieked and fled—oh! God, I saw
  The face—and that was mine.

Robert Burness.

123

THE SWORD OF SURPRISE

Sunder me from my bones, O sword of God,
Till they stand stark and strange as do the trees;
That I whose heart goes up with the soaring woods
May marvel as much as these.

Sunder me from my blood that in the dark
I hear that red ancestral river run,
Like branching buried floods that find the sea
But never see the sun.

Give me miraculous eyes to see my eyes,
Those rolling mirrors made alive in me,
Terrible crystal more incredible
Than all the things they see.

Sunder me from my soul, that I may see
The sins like streaming wounds, the life's brave
     beat;
Till I shall save myself, as I would save
A stranger in the street.

Gilbert Keith Chesterton.

THE HAPPY TREE

There was a bright and happy tree;
  The wind with music laced its boughs;
Thither across the houseless sea
  Came singing birds to house.

Men grudged the tree its happy eves,
  Its happy dawns of eager sound;
So all that crowd and tower of leaves
  They levelled with the ground.

They made an upright of the stem,
  A cross-piece of a bough they made:
No shadow of their deed on them
  The fallen branches laid.

But blithely, since the year was young,
  When they a fitting hill did find,
There on the happy tree they hung
  The Saviour of mankind.

Gerald Gould.

THE CAPTIVE LION

Thou that in fury with thy knotted tail
Hast made this iron floor thy beaten drum;
That now in silence walks thy little space—
Like a sea-captain—careless what may come:

What power has brought your majesty to this,
Who gave those eyes their dull and sleepy look;
Who took the lightning out, and from thy throat
The thunder when the whole wide forest shook?

It was that man who went again, alone,
Into thy forest dark—Lord, he was brave!
That man a fly has killed, whose bones are left
Unburied till an earthquake digs his grave.

W. H. Davies.

A CHANGE OF VIEW

They cut the trees, they dug the mains,
They trampled all the meadow way;
Left not a blade of daisied grass
To lay cool hands upon the day.

A cry floats in the stifled air,
The anguish of some wild, dumb thing;
In muted misery caged and caught,
While the green earth yet glows with Spring.

Now red bricks flaunt their insolence
Like tawdry women of the town;
Leering with cheap impertinence,
Tricked out to please in garish gown.

And where was once blue space of Heaven,
New-painted, horrid windows glare;
Making a mock of beauty gone,
Like empty eyes, that stare and stare.

S. Marguerite Goode.

127

THE STRANGER

Two dismal lines of bricked monotony,
A straggling weedy growth of chimney-pots,
A crazy thoroughfare, with little clots
And pools of oozy slime; no greenery,
And here no happy flowers shalt thou see;
No summer fruits, no sun-burnt apricots;
Save these, these withered frail forget-me-nots,
The little stunted babes of Poverty.

There came one walking down this silent street
Whose head with many cruel thorns was crowned,
In his right hand he held outstretched a wreath.
And where he walked with naked bleeding feet
There was no voice of birds, nor any sound,
And by his smile I knew that he was Death.

W. A. Lee.

RONDEL OF LONDON

To-day I spake with souls that journeyed by.
Here in the street they touched me as they passed.
Sorrow and Hope and Terror flying fast,
Life soon to bud, or, withering, soon to die.

And many more with troubled, speechless eye
Into my heart their timeless question cast.
To-day I spake with souls that journeyed by.
Here in the street they touched me as they passed.

The spires consumed in sunset, ceaselessly
The traffic surged with sob and trumpet blast.
Dusty, ensnared, immortal, driven fast
They raised their faces to the evening sky.—
To-day I spake with souls that journeyed by.

Lucy Lyttelton.

ON A HOUSE BEING PULLED DOWN

Against the sky the house uplifts
A skeleton, whence paper-drifts
A tattered testimony bear
That men lived there.

There they in fierce embrace were sown
And there they strove and grieved alone,
Till, gaping-mouthed and sightless-eyed,
Alone they died.

Upon each old enkindled grate
Looking, I seem to violate
Some hour of bitterness lived through
That no man knew.

I shrink as one that unawares
Has chanced upon a soul that bares
A nakedness, whereon may pry
Each passer-by.

J. Slingsby Roberts.

POINTS OF VIEW

The Caveman looked at the Forest
And knew that it was good:
Many kinds of trees grew there
And each had different wood.

Oak, that was tough and would not yield,
With branches stiff and stub;
Ash that would rive and make good stones
For hunting spear or club.

Holly, milk-white and bitter-hard,
That keenest edge would turn;
Willow one could twist like rope;
Pine that was good to burn.

Elder and hawthorn, bending yew,
Frow elm and bark-grained beech.
Every kind of tree he knew
And had a use for each.

The Caveman looked at the Forest
And knew what harbored there,
What fowls and beasts were good to eat,
Or had good skins to wear.

131

He knew each furred and feathered thing
That still in greenwood goes,
The mammoths and great hornèd beasts
That earth no longer knows—

The Caveman looked at the Forest
And trembled as he stood:
For gods and demons moved within
The dim mysterious wood:

God of tall tree and god of brake,
God of bush and brier;
The Caveman knew and feared them all
And shivered by his fire—

The Caveman looked at the Forest
Mysterious dim and high—
And many uncouth things he saw;
But naught so queer as I.

As I, who at the forest
Gaze hard, nor see the wood:
I see the Caveman by his cave,
I stand where once he stood.

I see the Caveman by his cave,
Finding his soul in prayer.
I see the Caveman by his cave,
Who never saw me there.

I see the Caveman by his cave,
I see the years between:

The dim mysterious teeming years
Where always Man has been.

I see the Caveman by his cave
As at the wood he peers;
I see the devils and the gods
Of twice ten thousand years—

A dazed bewildered thing I stand
Confused by memories—
Who scarcely can tell oak from ash,
Nor see the wood—for trees.

Kenneth H. Ashley.

CHILD

What wind is this across the roofs so softly makes
his way,
That hardly makes the wires to sing, or soaring
smoke to sway?

WIND

I am a weary southern wind that blows the livelong
day
Over the stones of Babylon,
Babylon, Babylon,
The ruined walls of Babylon, all fallen in decay.

Oh, I have blown o'er Babylon when royal was her
state,
When fifty men in gold and steel kept watch at
every gate,
When merchant-men and boys and maids thronged
early by and late
Under the gates of Babylon,
Babylon, Babylon,
The marble gates of Babylon, when Babylon was
great.

CHILD

Good weary wind, a little while pray let your course
be stayed,
And tell me of the talk they held and what the
people said,
The funny folk of Babylon before that they were
dead,
That walked abroad in Babylon,
Babylon, Babylon,
Before the towers of Babylon along the ground
were laid.

WIND

The folk that walked in Babylon, they talked of
wind and rain,
Of ladies' looks, of learned books, of merchants'
loss and gain,
How such-an-one loved such-a-maid that loved him
not again
(For maids were fair in Babylon,
Babylon, Babylon),
Also the poor in Babylon of hunger did complain.

CHILD

But this is what the people say as on their way they
go,
Under my window in the street, I heard them down
below.

135

WIND

What other should men talk about five thousand
years ago?
For men they were in Babylon,
Babylon, Babylon,
That now are dust in Babylon I scatter to-and-fro.

Lucy Lyttelton.

THE SPHINX

Ere days were days upon the earth
The Lord Almighty laid His hand.
I rose an everlasting hill,
And round my feet I felt the sand.
I felt upon my sightless brows
The child-winds leaning in their play,
Felt the first ripple of the Nile
Slip through my stones its seaward way.

Some came and shaped me brows and breast.
They gave me hearing, lips and eyes.
I heard the clanging of their gongs,
Smelt savor of their sacrifice.
I saw the kings in golden prows
Row with the flood to crown or bride,
I heard the wailing when they came
Back to the tomb, against the tide.

There passed a word between the winds.
They stirred the plains beyond the West.
The sands rose high behind my head,
The sands surged up against my breast.
The two waves meeting on my brows,
I waited, hidden in my place,

137

Till man remembered me again
And swept the sand from off my face.

Now Nile is far, and knows me not,
The desert sands remorseless rise,
My head is battered by the men
That used to make me sacrifice.
I lift my smitten brows and wait.
Men pass as prints of summer rain.
Nile will remember and return
To flow before my feet again.

Lucy Lyttelton.

WAR SONG OF THE SARACENS

We are they who come faster than fate: we are
    they who ride early or late:
We storm at your ivory gate: Pale Kings of the
    Sunset, beware!
Not on silk nor on samite we lie, not in curtained
    solemnity die
Among women who chatter and cry, and children
    who mumble a prayer.
But we sleep by the ropes of the camp, and we rise
    with a shout, and we tramp
With the sun or the moon for a lamp, and the spray
    of the wind in our hair.

From the lands where the elephants are, to the forts
    of Merou and Balghar,
Our steel we have brought and our star to shine on
    the ruins of Rum.
We have marched from the Indus to Spain, and by
    God we will go there again;
We have stood on the shore of the plain where the
    Waters of Destiny boom.
A mart of destruction we made at Jalula where men
    were afraid,

For death was a difficult trade, and the sword was
    a broker of doom;

And the Spear was a Desert Physician who cured
    not a few of ambition,
And drave not a few to perdition with medicine
    bitter and strong:
And the shield was a grief to the fool and as bright
    as a desolate pool,
And as straight as the rock of Stamboul when their
    cavalry thundered along:
For the coward was drowned with the brave when
    our battle sheered up like a wave,
And the dead to the desert we gave, and the glory to
    God in our song.

James Elroy Flecker.

THE MARCH

I heard a voice that cried, "Make way for those
    who died!"
And all the coloured crowd like ghosts at morning
    fled;
And down the waiting road, rank after rank there
    strode
In mute and measured march a hundred thousand
    dead.

A hundred thousand dead, with firm and noiseless
    tread,
All shadowy-grey yet solid, with faces grey and
    ghast,
And by the house they went, and all their brows
    were bent
Straight forward; and they passed, and passed, and
    passed, and passed.

But O there came a place, and O there came a face,
That clenched my heart to see it, and sudden turned
    my way;
And in the Face that turned I saw two eyes that
    burned,
Never-forgotten eyes, and they had things to say.

Like desolate stars they shone one moment, and
    were gone
And I sank down and put my arms across my head,
And felt them moving past, nor looked to see the
    last,
In steady silent march, our hundred thousand dead.

J. C. Squire.

A FALLEN SOLDIER

Hope held his hand and ran with him together.
Despair, the coward, at their coming fled.
Like a young ram, he shook his hornèd head,
And broke away from his restraining tether.
He loved the sea, he loved the cleansing flame;
No woman yet, his heart was all too young;
Over the plain of life his heart was flung,
Seeking for jeopardies that he might tame.
He cloaked his faith with laughter, but his faith
Was certain, as his confidence was gay,
And laughing went he, till on his last day
His hands stretched out to life were clasped by
    death.

                V. Sackville-West.

ELEGY

(For J. N., died of wounds, October, 1916)

So you are dead. We lived three months together,
    But in these years how absence can divide!
We did not meet again. I wonder whether
    You thought of me at all before you died.

There in that whirl of unaccustomed faces,
    Strange, friendless, ill, I found in you a friend—
And then at last in these divided places,
    For you in France and here for me the end.

For friendship's memory was short and faithless
    And time went by that will not come again,
And you are dead of wounds and I am scatheless
    Save as my heart has sorrowed for my slain.

I wonder whether you were long in dying,
    Where, in what trench and under what dim star,
With drawn face on the clayey bottom lying,
    While still the untiring guns cried out afar.

I might have been with you, I might have seen you
    Reel to the shot with blank and staring eye,

144

I might have held you up. . . . I might have been
    you
  And lain instead of you where now you lie.

Here in our quietude strange fancy presses,
  Dark thoughts of woe upon the empty brain,
And fills the streets and the pleasant wildernesses
  With forms of death and ugly shapes of pain.

You are long dead. A year is nearly over,
  But still your voice leaps out again amid
The tangled memories that lie and cover
  With countless trails what then we said and did.

And still in waking dreams I sit and ponder
  Pleasures that were and, as my working brain
Deeper in revery will stray and wander,
  I think that I shall meet with you again

And make my plans and half arrange the meeting,
  And half think out the words that will be said
After the first brief, careless, pleasant greet-
    ing . . .
  Then suddenly I remember you are dead.

Edward Shanks.

TO GERMANY

You are blind like us. Your hurt no man designed,
And no man claimed the conquest of your land.
But, gropers both through fields of thought confined,
We stumble and we do not understand.
You only saw your future bigly planned,
And we, the tapering paths of our own mind,
And in each other's dearest ways we stand,
And hiss and hate, and the blind fight the blind.
When it is peace, then we may view again
With new-won eyes each other's truer form,
And wonder. Grown more loving-kind and warm,
We'll grasp firm hands and laugh at the old pain,
When it is peace. But, until peace, the storm,
The darkness, and the thunder and the rain.

Charles Hamilton Sorley.

ALIEN ENEMIES

(The German mother speaks to the English mother)

On the cold frontier-line of death
I won my man-child blood and breath:
At a great price, in gulfs of night,
Purchased the morning for his sight,
And in a silence big with fear
Fore-wrought the musics he should hear.

And you?—ah, who should know but I
The wings of death that beat so nigh,
The deathly dark, the deathly dews,
The soul that will not yet refuse,
And all you risked, and all you paid,
When out of you your son was made?

Your son and mine in love were bred,
Your son and mine in hate are dead,
Yet never hated, never knew
The sense of what they had to do,
But perished, brother slain by brother,
Who might as well have loved each other.
The happy hands, too good to put

147

To the red business of the brute;
The candid eyes that death's release
Found peopled with my dreams of peace;
The hope beneath the heart that grew—
Ah, who should know them if not you?

Dear mother of a murdered son,
Ours is the end by us begun!
Ours is the strength the guns called up,
And ours it is to drink the cup
Of childless days, of childless years,
Salt with the taste of blood and tears.

Dear murdered mother!—still to die
The women's regiments go by:
No music of the march for them,
And for their souls no requiem,
When, 'mid the screaming of the guns,
The mothers perish in their sons.

And we are foes, or so they tell me—
But in the wonder that befell me,
When, solitary soldier, I
Fought for the life so soon to die—
When out of night I brought, I won,
My morning-star, my little son—
When at the utter risk and cost
I gained the solace I have lost—

When underneath my opening eyes
Lay that which now all altered lies—

148

When to my warm and passionate breast
I held the limbs now cold in rest —
I knew one peace that shall not end,
And every mother for my friend.

Gerald Gould.

PIERROT AT THE WAR

The leaden years have dragged themselves away;
  The blossoms of the world lie all dashed down
And flattened by the hurricane of death:
The roses fallen, and their fragrant breath
  Has passed beyond our senses—and we drown
Our tragic thoughts; confine them to the day.

Pierrot was happy here two years ago,
  Singing through all the summer-scented hours,
Dancing throughout the warm moon-haunted night.
Swan-like his floating sleeves, so long and white,
  Sailed the blue waters of the dusk. Wan flowers,
Like moons, perfumed the crystal valley far below.

But now these moonlit sleeves lie on the ground,
  Trampled and torn from many a deadly fight.
With fingers clenched, and face a mask of stone,
He gazes at the sky—left all alone—
  Grimacing under every rising light:
His body waits the peace his soul has found.

Osbert Sitwell.

150

LEPANTO

White founts falling in the Courts of the sun,
And the Soldan of Byzantium is smiling as they
run;
There is laughter like the fountains in the face of
all men feared,
It stirs the forest darkness, the darkness of his
beard,
It curls the blood-red crescent, the crescent of his
lips,
For the inmost sea of all the earth is shaken with
his ships.
They have dared the white republics up the capes
of Italy,
They have dashed the Adriatic round the Lion of
the Sea,
And the Pope has cast his arms abroad for agony
and loss,
And called the kings of Christendom for swords
about the Cross.
The cold queen of England is looking in the
glass;
The shadow of the Valois is yawning at the
Mass;

From evening isles fantastical rings faint the
Spanish gun,
And the Lord upon the Golden Horn is laughing in
the sun.

Dim drums throbbing, in the hills half heard,
Where only on a nameless throne a crownless prince
has stirred,
Where, risen from a doubtful seat and half attainted
stall,
The last Knight of Europe takes weapons from the
wall,
The last and lingering troubadour to whom no bird
has sung,
That once went singing southward when all the
world was young.
In that enormous silence, tiny and unafraid,
Comes up along a winding road the noise of the
Crusade.
Strong gongs groaning as the guns boom far,
Don John of Austria is going to the war,
Stiff flags straining in the night-blasts cold
In the gloom black-purple, in the glint old-gold,
Torchlight crimson on the copper kettle-drums,
Then the tuckets, then the trumpets, then the
cannon, and he comes.
Don John laughing in the brave beard curled,
Spurning of his stirrups like the thrones of all the
world,
Holding his head up for a flag of all the free.
Love-light of Spain—hurrah!

Death-light of Africa!
Don John of Austria
Is riding to the sea.

Mahound is his Paradise above the evening star.
(*Don John of Austria is going to the war.*)
He moves a mighty turban on the timeless houri's
    knees,
His turban that is woven of the sunsets and the seas.
He shakes the peacock gardens as he rises from his
    ease,
And he strides among the tree-tops and is taller
    than the trees,
And his voice through all the garden is a thunder
    sent to bring
Black Azrael and Ariel and Ammon on the wing.
Giants and the Genii,
Multiplex of wing and eye,
Whose strong obedience broke the sky
When Solomon was king.

They rush in red and purple from the red clouds of
    the morn,
From temples where the yellow gods shut up their
    eyes in scorn;
They rise in green robes roaring from the green hells
    of the sea
Where fallen skies and evil hues and eyeless crea-
    tures be;
On them the sea-valves cluster and the grey sea-
    forests curl,

153

Splashed with a splendid sickness, the sickness of
the pearl;
They swell in sapphire smoke out of the blue cracks
of the ground,—
They gather and they wonder and give worship to
Mahound.
And he saith, "Break up the mountains where the
hermit-folk can hide,
And sift the red and silver sands lest bone of saint
abide,
And chase the Giaours flying night and day, not
giving rest,
For that which was our trouble comes again out of
the west.
We have set the seal of Solomon on all things under
sun,
Of knowledge and of sorrow and endurance of
things done,
But a noise is in the mountains, in the mountains,
and I know
The voice that shook our palaces—four hundred
years ago:
It is he that saith not 'Kismet'; it is he that knows
not Fate;
It is Richard, it is Raymond, it is Godfrey at the
gate!
It is he whose loss is laughter when he counts the
wager worth,
Put down your feet upon him, that our peace be
on the earth."
For he heard guns groaning, and he heard guns jar,

(Don John of Austria is going to the war.)
Sudden and still—hurrah!
Bolt from Iberia!
Don John of Austria
Is gone by Alcalar.

St. Michael's on his mountain in the sea-roads of
    the north
(Don John of Austria is girt and going forth.)
Where the grey seas glitter and the sharp tides shift
And the sea-folk labor and the red sails lift.
He shakes his lance of iron and he claps his wings
    of stone;
The noise is gone through Normandy; the noise is
    gone alone;
The North is full of tangled things and texts and
    aching eyes
And dead is all the innocence of anger and surprise,
And Christian killeth Christian in a narrow dusty
    room,
And Christian dreadeth Christ that hath a newer
    face of doom,
And Christian hateth Mary that God kissed in
    Galilee,
But Don John of Austria is riding to the sea.
Don John calling through the blast and the eclipse,
Crying with the trumpet, with the trumpet of his
    lips,
Trumpet that sayeth *ha!*
  Domino gloria!

Don John of Austria
Is shouting to the ships.

King Philip's in his closet with the Fleece about his
neck
(*Don John of Austria is armed upon the deck.*)
The walls are hung with velvet that is black and
soft as sin,
And little dwarfs creep out of it and little dwarfs
creep in.
He holds a crystal phial that has colors like the
moon,
He touches, and it tingles, and he trembles very
soon,
And his face is as a fungus of a leprous white and
grey,
Like plants in the high houses that are shuttered
from the day,
And death is in the phial and the end of noble work,
But Don John of Austria has fired upon the Turk.
Don John's hunting and his hounds have bayed—
Booms away past Italy the rumor of his raid.
Gun upon gun, ha! ha!
Gun upon gun, hurrah!
Don John of Austria
Has loosed the cannonade.

The Pope was in his chapel before day or battle
broke,
(*Don John of Austria is hidden in the smoke.*)

The hidden room in man's house where God sits all
    the year,
The secret window whence the world looks small
    and very dear.
He sees as in a mirror on the monstrous twilight sea
The crescent of his cruel ships whose name is
    mystery;
They fling great shadows foe-wards, making Cross
    and Castle dark,
They veil the plumèd lions on the galleys of St.
    Mark;
And above the ships are palaces of brown, black-
    bearded chiefs,
And below the ships are prisons where, with multi-
    tudinous griefs,
Christian captives sick and sunless, all a laboring
    race repines
Like a race in sunken cities, like a nation in the
    mines.
They are lost like slaves that sweat, and in the skies
    of morning hung
The stairways of the tallest gods when tyranny was
    young.
They are countless, voiceless, hopeless as those
    fallen or fleeing on
Before the high Kings' horses in the granite of
    Babylon.
And many a one grows witless in his quiet room in
    hell
Where a yellow face looks inward through the
    lattice of his cell,

And he finds his God forgotten, and he seeks no
    more a sign—
(*But Don John of Austria has burst the battle
    line!*)
Don John pounding from the slaughter-painted
    poop,
Purpling all the ocean like a bloody pirate's sloop,
Scarlet running over on the silvers and the golds,
Breaking of the hatches up and bursting of the
    holds,
Thronging of the thousands up that labor under sea,
White for bliss and blind for sun and stunned for
    liberty.
Vivat Hispania!
Domino Gloria!
Don John of Austria
Has set his people free!

Cervantes on his galley sets the sword back in the
    sheath
(*Don John of Austria rides honored with a wreath.*)
And he sees across a weary land a straggling road in
    Spain,
Up which a lean and foolish knight forever rides in
    vain,
And he smiles, but not as Sultans smile, and settles
    back the blade . . .
(*But Don John of Austria rides home from the
    Crusade.*)

             Gilbert Keith Chesterton.

THE HAMMERS

Noise of hammers once I heard,
Many hammers, busy hammers,
Beating, shaping, night and day,
Shaping, beating dust and clay
To a palace; saw it reared;
Saw the hammers laid away.

And I listened, and I heard
Hammers beating, night and day,
In the palace newly reared,
Beating it to dust and clay:
Other hammers, muffled hammers,
Silent hammers of decay.

Ralph Hodgson.

ALTER EGO

Who is it that I drag about;
This carping ever present thing,
Who splits my purpose, breeding doubt?
Is he my subject or my king?
    Body and soul we well may be,
    But which am 'I' and which is 'he'?

Some day, they say, I shall escape,
And looking down from the high sky,
Shall see below in finite shape
Divorced by death, this other I:
    And know on that transcendant day
    That I was spirit, he was clay.

Yet—what if mine the part to lie
Cast off, out worn, and viewed with loathing,
To rot where he has flung me by,
Glad to be rid of his smirched clothing?
    If he were greater, none the less,
    And I below *his* consciousness?

Kenneth H. Ashley.

PULVIS ET UMBRA

Along the crowded streets I walk and think
How I, a shadow, pace among the shades,
For I and all men seem to be unreal:
Foam that the seas of God which cover all
Cast on the air a moment, shadows thrown
In moving westward by the Moon of Death.

Oh, shall it set at last, that orb of Death?
May any morning follow? As I think,
From one surmise upon another thrown,
My very thoughts appear to me as shades—
Shades, like the prisoning self that bounds them all,
Shades, like the transient world, and as unreal.

But other hours there be when I, unreal,
When only I, vague in a conscious Death,
Move through the mass of men unseen by all;
I move along their ways, I feel and think,
Yet am more light than echoes, or the shades
That hide me, from their stronger bodies thrown.

And better moments come when, overthrown
All round me, lie the ruins of the unreal
And momentary world, as thin as shades;

When I alone, triumphant over Death,
Eternal, vast, fill with the thoughts I think,
And with my single soul the frame of all.

Ah, for a moment could I grasp it all
Ah, could but I (poor wrestler often thrown)
Once grapple with the truth, oh then, I think,
Assured of which is living, which unreal,
I would not murmur though among the shades
My lot were cast, among the shades and Death.

"One thing is true," I said, "and that is Death,"
And yet it may be God disproves it all;
And Death may be a passage from the shades,
And films on our beclouded senses thrown;
And Death may be a step beyond the Unreal
Towards the Thought that answers all I think.

In vain I think. O moon-like thought of Death,
All is unreal beneath thee, uncertain all,
Dim moon-ray thrown along a world of shades!

A. Mary F. Robinson.

THE SOUL OF MAN

In the soul of man there are many voices,
  That silence wakens and sound restrains:
A song of love, that the soul rejoices,
  With windy music, and murmuring rains;

A song of light, when the dawn arises,
  And earth lies shining, and wet with dew;
And life goes by, in a myriad guises,
  Under a heaven of stainless blue.

The willows, bending over the river,
  Where the water ripples between the reeds,
Where the shadows sway, and the pale lights quiver
  On floating lily, and flowing weeds,

Have whispering voices, soft as showers
  Of April falling on upland lawns,
On the nodding harebell, and pale wind-flowers,
  Through silver evens, and golden dawns.

But softer than love, and deeper than longing
  Are the sweet, frail voices of drifting ghosts;
In the soul of man they are floating, thronging
  As wind-blown petals, pale, flickering hosts.

Frederic Manning.

TO KEATS

On a magical morning, with twinkling feet,
And a song at his lips that was strange and sweet,
Somebody new came down the street
   To the world's derision and laughter.

Now he is dumb with no more to say,
Now he is dead and taken away,
Silent and still and leading the way,
   And the world come tumbling after.

Lord Dunsany.

THE COMING POET

"Is it far to the town?" said the poet,
As he stood 'neath the groaning vane,
And the warm lights shimmered silver
On the skirts of the windy rain.
"These are those who call me," he pleaded,
"And I'm wet and travel sore."
But nobody spoke from the shelter,
And he turned from the bolted door.

And they wait in the town for the poet
With stones at the gates, and jeers,
But away on the wolds of distance
In the blue of a thousand years
He sleeps with the age that knows him,
In the clay of the unborn, dead,
Rest at his weary insteps,
Fame at his crumbled head.

Francis Ledwidge.

TO ALL MINOR POETS

My brothers, who have plucked the flowers of
    rhyme
And strewn them on the highways thick and fast,
The blossoms of a moment that we cast
Shall lie forgotten for a long, long time:
Till all we said, and all we thought about
Grows quaint and strange, and all our life has past
For ever from the earth. And when at last
Some lover of old songs shall draw us out
From the great rubbish-heap of time, to please
His fancy with an age unlike his own,
And set us tenderly upon his shelves,
We shall be so transformed and overgrown
By subtle workings of the centuries,
I think that we shall hardly know ourselves.

Roger Heath.

THE FOOL

The madman wandering head in air
    About the mustard fields
Sees hosts of flying angels there
    With golden spears and shields;
The fool, the fool men pity and despise,
The brain-sick fool, with wonder stricken eyes.

He cannot hold his mind to earth,
    He lives in heaven all day;
Bright sunlit spirits in their mirth
    Flit round about his way.
The fool, the fool stands happy for an hour
To see an angel in a common flower.

He cannot see the wild-rose tree,
    He cannot see the stone;
Strange presences around him be,
    He never goes alone.
The fool, the fool who walks the lanes at night,
Feels a warm love enwrap him round like light.

He wanders where the poppies grow
    Red-flaming in the sun;
The racing winds against him blow,
    A living voice each one.—
The fool, the fool has wit enough to find
God's whisper in the passing of the wind.

E. G. Morice.

THE OLD

Surely they know, the old;
    The years have made them wise.
What secrets do they hold
    Within their tired eyes?

With many a differing tongue
    Long trained in wordy strife
Hear while they tell the young
    The mystery of life.

Some trod the road marked "Straight,"
    Scorning the pleasant plains.
Their love has changed to hate,
    Seeing their little gains.

Yet, envious, they would keep
    Their followers therein,
Mumbling in senile sleep
    "Death is the wage of sin."

Some chose the fairer way
    Where love and beauty rove.
Now, sick at heart, they say:
    "We know not Lust from Love,

"And Beauty mates with shame
   And early dreams have died.
What secret should we name?
   We know the world is wide."

And some have followed Truth:
   Shaking with cynic mirth
They croak: "Not here, O youth,
   Nor anywhere on earth."

Who toiled for fame or gold
   Speak tonelessly or slow:
"We? But we are not old;
   Our souls died long ago."

All yearn for life beyond
   The unknown gate of Death.
Yet, God, what men more fond
   Than old men of their breath?

O youth, they do not know!
   You tread a lonely road.
No other soul can show
   Where lies your soul's abode.

H. Ross.

REMORSE

Throughout her round of common days
She conquered selfish, vain desire,
And, fed from out her spirit's fire,
The lamp of service lit her ways.

And we who were her only care
In grief or laughter, ill or good,
We gave her little gratitude,
Of praise we left her unaware.

But when we knew that she was dead,
Then rose the unacknowledged years
Of toil before us, and our tears
Were bitter for the words unsaid.

The sun she loved, and singing birds
And blossoms on the summer trees,
She gained more gladness out of these
Than ever came from human words.

To-day the sun is on her grave,
But she is gone beyond the sun.
And does she know how late begun
We speak of her as good and brave?

With God we plead for this alone,
That she may know our long regret,
That she may hear the praises yet
Of hearts that hunger to atone.

Nancy Pollok.

LOVE'S MADNESS

Well, so it is: the thing I had
Was fit to make the world run mad:
It was a splendor so intense
It smote my sins to innocence,
And through men's mist of fears and lies
Clove one clear pathway to the skies.

Such was the race I might have run;
Such was the palm I might have won;
Such was the light, the flame, the flower:
And in a day and in an hour
I took it as not fit to take
And spent it for a woman's sake.

I cannot think she did not pay
The worth of any hour or day:
She could not know, she could not guess,
The world's loss or my loneliness,
But paid for all (O just and wise)
With the least laughter of her eyes.

And if an angel came in tears
And proffered me my wasted years,
And spread before my feet anew
The race to run, the deed to do,
With all things sweet and all things strange
—I would not change, I would not change!

Gerald Gould.

EMBARKMENT

Useless, and cast like seaweed on the shore,
Where children yet may find it in their play,
Lies my discarded Book of yesterday
(Of yesterday, and all that came before);
And only yesterday, I prized it more
Than nun her missal when she goes to pray,
And through its pages let my fancy stray
Among enchanted realms of mystic lore.

And often, with eyes kindling from the tale,
I seemed to view strange pageantries unfurl,
Bright phantom banners in a phantom breeze . . .
But that is past; and now, tumultuous seas
Shout to the far horizon, and I hurl
My ship upon the waters, and set sail.

Maisie Bell Whyte.

YOUTH'S IMMORTALITIES

The Abbey's three tall towers
　Behold the tides of men
Flow from their silent waters
　To seas beyond their ken;
They gazed on us, my brothers,
　And we were happy then.

Our footsteps, oh my brothers,
　In pleasant paths were set,
With pleasures to remember,
　And sorrows to forget,
Deep draughts of love and laughter,
　A cup without regret.

In days of joyous labor
　And golden leisure hours,
We spent the spring of living,
　Chequered with sun and showers,
And grew to manhood's measure
　Beneath the three grey towers.

Our battle still was distant
　And faint the drum and fife,
Yet we knew the flush of conquest
　And the virile joys of strife,
And fingers dimly groping
　Came near the key of life.

And bells on summer evenings,
　Like a peal of silver tears
For beauty sadly wandering
　Among the misty years,
Woke the stirring soul within us
　To speak of hopes and fears.

Hopes for life's great adventure,
　And for a world set free;
Fear in a dim foreknowledge
　Of wanderings to be,
Hearing on sunny uplands
　The sound of storm at sea.

And often, in hushed voices
　We talked the night away,
With speech of all the wonders
　That lie too deep for day,
Till morning faintly flushing
　Rose from her couch of grey.

Time is the strong destroyer
　Of most that Heaven sends,
And cherished treasures daily
　Draw to their destined ends,
But youth shall live for ever
　In the trusty grip of friends.

William Noel Hodgson.

THE MEETING

As I went through the ancient town,
  Long lost and found once more,
Oh, who is this in a green gown
  I knew so well of yore?

Veils of enchantment hid the place,
  Hung every street and square:
I felt the sea-wind in my face
  And ruffling in my hair.

Oh town I loved so well and lost,
  And find again with tears,
Your streets hold many a darling ghost
  And all the vanished years!

My heart went singing a low song,
  Glad to be home again.
But who is this comes blithe and young,
  Not feared of life but fain?

Oh, who is this comes cold as stone
  To my quick cry and call?
Of all the faces loved and flown
  I knew her best of all.

"Stay, you are . . ." Is she deaf and blind
  Or hath she quite forgot?
What chill is in the sun, the wind,
  Because she knows me not?

As I went down—my eyes were wet—
  Eager and stepping fast
That was my own sweet youth I met
  Who knew me not and passed.

Katherine Tynan.

IN THE GLOAMING

I   ABOVE

"In the gloaming—O! my Darling, when the lights
      are dim and low,
And the quiet shadows falling, softly come and
      softly go,
And the winds are sobbing faintly with a gentle
      unknown woe,
Will you think of me, and love me, as you once did,
      long ago?
    In the gloaming—O! my Darling,
    When the merry song is stilled,
    And your voices sink to whispers
    And the thought your heart has thrilled
    All day long 'neath jest and laughter
    Rises, and your eyes are filled
    With bitter tears for my last face,
    Think only of a trust fulfilled.
In the gloaming—O! my Darling, think not bitterly
      of me;
Though I passed away in silence, left you lonely,
      set you free:
For my heart was crushed with longing, what had
      been could never be,
It was best to leave you quickly, best for you and
      best for me."

"In the gloaming—O! my Darling, when the quiet
    shadows fall,
And my lone heart in its sadness seemeth achingly
    to call
To the sobbing winds that echo only deepening
    pain and thrall,
I will answer through life's darkness, trusting love
    to fathom all.
    In the gloaming, O! my Darling,
    Your brave trust shall be fulfilled
    Though I shrink beneath my smiling
    And my longing eyes are filled
    With those saddest tears that fall not,
    I shall rouse me as you willed,
    I shall bear me in life's working
    Nobly till my grief is stilled.
In the gloaming—O! my Darling, I shall think—
    not bitterly—
Of your passing from me silent, judging with true
    fealty
Love the highest and the purest in the silence to be
    strong,
Till beyond the gates we clasp each other freed
    from earthly wrong."

Meta Orred.

SONG

(From "Hassan")

How splendid in the morning glows the lily; with
    what grace he throws

His supplication to the rose: do roses nod the head,
    Yasmin?

But when the silver dove descends, I find the little
    flower of friends,

Whose very name that sweetly ends, I say when I
    have said, Yasmin.

The morning light is clear and cold; I dare not in
    that light behold

A whiter light, a deeper gold, a glory too far shed,
    Yasmin.

But when the deep red eye of day is level with the
    lone highway,

And some to Mecca turn to pray, and I toward thy
    bed, Yasmin.

Or when the wind beneath the moon is drifting like
    a soul aswoon,

And harping planets talk love's tune with milky
    wings outspread, Yasmin,

Shower down thy love, O burning bright! for one
    night or the other night

Will come the Gardener in white, and gathered
    flowers are dead, Yasmin!

James Elroy Flecker.

179

SONG

My love is like a dark tree
   Whose roots grow strong and deep;
And all day long, protectingly,
His wide arms fling the winds from me
Or sift the sun-gold gallantly
   For me to catch and keep.

My love is like a King's tree
   Royally flourishing;
And even his fallen leaves shall be
Rich patterns on the path of me,
When light fades from the utmost sea
   And birds forget to sing.

Maisie Bell Whyte.

SONG

Thoughts timorous as the swift deer's shadow pass
      Before your eyes,
Light as the breath that whispers in the grass
      And whispering dies.

Your mind is a blue dancing butterfly
      Beyond my reach;
A wild thing wheeling with the seagulls by
      A windy beach.

It is a long weed waving, dimly seen
      Beneath a stream;
A cuckoo calling in a wood between
      Waking and dream.

L. A. G. Strong.

TRIOLET

To lay upon thy quiet grave
I bring no flowers belovéd heart:
My fairest blooms I did not save
To lay upon thy quiet grave.
Love's blossoms unto thee I gave
Freely before thou didst depart.
To lay upon thy quiet grave.
I bring no flowers belovéd heart.

Bertha Annakin.

REFUGE

As in the tales of wonder, known of old,
Some mariner would find his heart's desire—
An island of pure peace, a town of gold
Set on the splendid hilltop, spire on spire;
And there, far from the long waves' lonely swell,
His anchored ship in harbor cool and deep,
This tired adventurer a space would dwell
Where waking held more dreams than mortal sleep;
So I have hours of wonder, when I gain
Your Presence; and your soul, remote and still,
Waits, an enchanted refuge from all pain,
But further than that city on the hill!
And I, storm tossed and weary, rest awhile,
As in the peace of that far, fairy isle.

Vera I. Arlett.

HAVEN

I have come home at last; the port is still
And evening winds foretell a deep, hushed night.
O, if you only knew how strong the will
That captained me, how faint and far the light!
Here, now at peace, I think of bitter seas,
With skies a hopeless black; mad winds that fled
Shrieking the storm's tormented ecstasies,
And darkened every light that lay ahead.
Yet lonely on my soul's long, level wave
The mornings rose, the yellow sunsets died;
And many were the un-named thoughts I gave
Into the soundless depth below that tide.
But now, the moorings of your peace hold fast,—
Most patient watcher, I am home at last.

Vera I. Arlett.

"BETWEEN"

I have not reached the other side of Care,
Nor felt the comfort of the sun-warmed air
And the soft breaths of those that flourish there.

I cannot tread the span that lies between;
My eyes are unaccustomed to the sheen,
My faltering feet to rainbow-bridged ravine.

Only I strain to see beyond this place
Your lips, your eyes, the Soul within your face,
That draws my Spirit into Infinite Space.

Joan Warburg.

ACHIEVEMENT

If we had sought adventurously the stars,
   Or snared some wandering angel with a song,
Or healed men's hearts of fear, the world of wars,
   Death of its sting, and love of half its wrong;

If we had lifted an imperious name
   Beyond the narrow bounds of mortal mood,
Fanning with the quick impulse of our fame
   The crawling moments of the multitude:—

Then were there cause for pride—*then* might we dare
   To claim some bright, extravagant reward
      Beyond the reach of Time.—Alas! our boast

Is only that one day was wholly fair,
   When beechen leaves cast patterns on green sward,
      —One day in Spring. All other days are lost.

Margaret Sackville.

THE BALLAD OF CAMDEN TOWN

I walked with Maisie long years back
  The streets of Camden town,
I splendid in my suit of black,
  And she divine in brown.

Hers was a proud and noble face,
  A secret heart, and eyes
Like water in a lonely place
  Beneath unclouded skies.

A bed, a chest, a faded mat,
  And broken chairs a few,
Were all we had to grace our flat
  In Hazel Avenue.

But I could walk to Hampstead Heath,
  And crown her head with daisies,
And watch the streaming world beneath,
  And men with other Maisies.

When I was ill and she was pale
  And empty stood our store,
She left the latchkey on its nail,
  And saw me nevermore.

Perhaps she cast herself away
    Lest both of us should drown:
Perhaps she feared to die, as they
    Who die in Camden Town.

What came of her? The bitter nights
    Destroy the rose and lily,
And souls are lost among the lights
    Of painted Piccadilly.

What came of her? The river flows
    So deep and wide and stilly,
And waits to catch the fallen rose
    And clasp the broken lily.

I dream she dwells in London still
    And breathes the evening air,
And often walk to Primrose Hill
    And hope to meet her there.

Once more together we will live,
    For I will find her yet:
I have so little to forgive;
    So much, I can't forget.

James Elroy Flecker.

CROSS ROADS

Where two roads meet she waits, her straining eyes
Bent on the far horizon. On one hand
The way winds through a pleasant, smiling land
And Wisdom beckons there. The other lies
Mid realms of troubled splendor: summits rise
In storm-swept purity: Love takes his stand
Upon a chasm's brink. His eyes command
But he keeps silence. Still she waits and sighs.
Since God made man we women thus have stood,
With bursting heart, and weary, weary brain
To make that choice which falls to womanhood.
The way of ease or rugged path of pain?
Ah see, her choice is made Her lips respond
To Love's embrace. She will not look beyond.

E. M. Kelly.

IF BEAUTY CAME TO YOU

If Beauty came to you,
  Ah, would you know her grace,
And could you in your shadowed prison view
  Unscathed her face?

Stepping as noiselessly
  As moving moth-wings, so
Might she come suddenly to you or me
  And we not know.

Amid these clangs and cries,
  Alas, how should we hear
The shy, dim-woven music of her sighs
  As she draws near,

Threading through monstrous, black
  Uncharitable hours,
Where the soul shapes its own abhorred rack
  Of wasted powers?

William Kean Seymour.

THE BLACKBIRD

Evening over fields of cloud
  In sombre beauty came,
Washing the slumbering trees with mist
  And the tall spires with flame.

Then from one of the still trees
  Like drops that run along
The glossy faces of green leaves,
  Fell a blackbird's song:

And Memory opened dreaming eyes
  And the pale ghosts stirred,
And heaven and earth went down before
  The soft note of a bird.

For as the hidden blackbird spoke
  Out of the leafy tree,
One long and shining wave-crest broke
  Along a secret sea.

Martin Armstrong.

LINES ON A BULLFINCH, FREED

Who once was held in durance vile
Now flits among the leafy trees;
Nor wit, nor will, nor food, nor guile
May lure him back to captive ease.

Where finches throng in buoyant flight
He dips and rises with the rest,
And the warm amber of the light
Flushes the ruby of his breast.

Among the cool of willow sedge,
Where grasses droop a tawny seed,
We mark him by the river's edge
His light weight balanced on a reed.

And it may be the while we watch
In silence from a drifting boat,
Hid in the leaves our ear shall catch
The small perfection of his note.

Then let him thieve the garden still,
A blessèd bird beyond our reach,
With all the ebon of his bill
Bright with the nectar of the peach.

And through a wealth of ransomed days
Let him uplift his wings to fly,
And let his be the woodland ways
And the wide places of the sky.

Pamela Tennant.

HUNTING SONG

The hunt is up, the hunt is up,
It sounds from hill to hill,
It pierces to the secret place
Where we are lying still,
And one of us the quarry is,
And one of us must go
When through the arches of the wood
We hear the dread horn blow.

A huntsman bold is Master Death,
And reckless does he ride,
And terror's hounds with bleeding fangs
Go baying at his side.
And will it be a milk white doe
Or little dappled fawn,
Or will it be an antlered stag
Must face the icy dawn?

Or will it be a golden fox
Must leap from out his lair,
Or where the trailing shadows pass
A merry romping hare?
The hunt is up, the horn is loud
By plain and covert side,

And one must run alone, alone,
When Death abroad does ride.

But idle 'tis to crouch in fear
Since Death will find you out.
Then up and hold your head erect
And pace the wood about,
And swim the stream, and leap the wall,
And race the starry mead,
Nor feel the bright teeth in your flank
Till they be there indeed.

For in the secret hearts of men
Are peace and joy at one,
There is a pleasant land where stalks
No darkness in the sun,
And through the arches of the wood
Do break like silver foam
Young laughter and the noise of flutes
And voices singing home.

Sylvia Lynd.

SEA CAVES

I came at the ebb of the calling tide
  Where wandered surges roam,
And a Dead Thing paced with me side by side
  And laughed at the whispering foam;
He flung the ghost of a broken toy
  At the heels of the moaning sea,
And his laugh was the laugh of a buried joy
  That broke the heart of me.

I fled the length of the gleaming sands
  And the Dead Thing went before,
Till I stayed at the edge of the Sorrowful Lands
  Where the black rocks leave the shore;
And all around was the soft sweet flood
  And the lap of the crooning swell,
On the farmost rock the Dead Thing stood
  And chanted the Dead Thing's spell;

Till away beyond a mermaid sang,
  On the crest of the waiting sea,
And shoreward, shoreward her music rang
  Like a dream of harmony.
For its lilt was ever of green sea-caves
  Where fossilled memories lie,

And peace is over the sand-strewn graves,
   And Dead Things really die.

I crept and gazed at the sea-caves green
   As I knelt at the Dead Thing's side
With a thousand fathoms of peace between
   And the lure of the calling tide.
And there as the sea-maid ceased to sing
   On the crest of the waiting sea
I saw her stand where the sea-weeds swing
   Round the graves of memory.

Madeline Nightingale.

THE GREAT SHIPS

I wonder if the great ships
Are coming o'er the bar
With the West Wind in their rigging,
From unseen lands afar,
And if they slowly sail on
The rayless waters flowing
By the gates of a city I love well,
And where I would be going.

For I am as the great ships
And on the tide of life
Go forth to unknown places
And ne'er find rest but strife,
And in a human ocean
'Mid isles of brick and stone,
Past ports and lands I know not,
I sail through seas unknown.

I wonder if the great ships
Are crowding into port,
With mournful sirens wailing
As though from sea they brought
The terror of their conflict
Which holds them as they creep
From highways of the ocean
And wonders of the deep.

197

For I am as the great ships,
And sailing in a sea
Where chartless souls are moving
On human tides—to me
Comes thought of lands of twilight
And ports of rest where lie
The weary ships unchartered
Beneath an evening sky.

I wonder if the great ships
Creep up at break of dawn,
The seagulls round their rigging,
Grey-winged, with cries forlorn;
Those ships and birds sail ever
Through dreams of mine that are
Of lone lands in the twilight
And the sunset o'er the bar

Cecil Roberts.

A SUMMER NIGHT

The crescent moon sinks slowly down
And, seeming to my fancy's eye
A silver gallery in the sky,
Hangs low above the sleeping town;

Hangs low above the little bay,
Touching the dancing waves with light,
Where once on such a summer night
Perchance some Viking warship lay.

Far out with measured stroke and slow,
A boat is drawing to the shore;
I hear the creaking of the oar
And distant voices deep and low.

Then closing eyes I seem to hear
The old sea-rover's boats that slip
From out the shadow of the ship
In some old, long-forgotten year,

When towering o'er the moonlit deep
Came the long dragons of the North,
And the fierce sons of Thor stole forth
To fall upon the town in sleep.

Here where the quiet moonbeams stray
Across the beach and up the street,

Was heard the tread of sudden feet
With clash of steel and war horns' bray.

The startled watchman, catching breath
Even with the white blade at his throat,
Blew loud and clear one warning note,—
And found his swift reward in death.

Then shriek and shout and clash of brand,
Wild cries of triumph and despair,
Borne on the fragrant summer air
Echoed about the shuddering land;

Echoed, and sank and died away,
And silence held the night again,
Save for the oarsmen's wild refrain
As the long ship swept down the bay.

Across the starlit silence drew
A formless shadow, and below
Pale tongues of light shot to and fro
Now gleaming red, now ghastly blue,

Till flushed the sky with lurid red
As leaped to heaven the sudden fire,
Wrapping in one vast funeral pyre
The blood-stained streets and quiet dead.

And still the waves went murmuring
The pebbled beaches far along
That wonderful and world-old song
Which here to-night I hear them sing.

.   .   .   .

The moon is gone, a rosy gleam
Is brightening in the Eastern sky,
The blood and flame of days gone by
Have vanished with my waking dream.

                    Duncan J. Robertson.

A BALLAD OF DREAMLAND

To-Night in Dreamland who can rest?
  We hear on the night wind falling,
Over the hills in the dim, dark West,
  The horn of a huntsman calling.
"Follow!" the horn of the huntsman cries;
  On the wind over plain and hollow
A voice from the tarn where Echo lies
  Dreamily answers, "Follow!"

We hear the far-off horn, we come,
  Into the forest sweepeth
The wild white chase of waters dumb
  Where the fern and the hemlock sleepeth.
Who knows the form of the thing that flies?
  Hath it feet? Hath it wings like a swallow?
Who cares? The horn of the hunter cries
  To the shadowy huntsmen, "Follow!"

The third cock crows, the dawn wind blows,
  The beams of morning quiver;
Down vale and glade the huntsmen fade
  Like mists upon the river.
Whilst o'er the streams and hills of dreams
  Die horn and hunting halloa,
Far, far away where night nor day
  Nor hound nor horse, may follow.

Henry De Vere Stacpoole.

THE BIRD ON YGDRASIL

In the blowing tops of Ygdrasil,
  Over the Astral sea,
My spirit like a splendid bird
  Sings in infinity.
Sometimes I hear the psalm he sings:
  With baby words I try
To sing in time that boundless rhyme
  Beneath this little sky.

On the dazzling trees of Ygdrasil,
  In God's vast summer day—
Where sits the seven-horned triple sun
  That lights the Milky Way,
My spirit on the blossomed bough
  In sapphire climes unknown,
'Mid streaming glory, gazes down
  On this dull flesh and bone.

Sometimes I feel his favouring smile
  On that high perch afar,
And smiling up the bowery sky
  I hail him from my star,
And ponder in this puny world
  With pigmy thoughts of mine
How this poor gipsy-sprite dare claim
  A relative so fine.

On the dizzy heights of Ygdrasil
  In my lord's boundless gaze
The earth looks like a diamond bright
  With its twinkling years and days:
Oh! dearest of the petalled stars
  That dance on all the tree
To him this sparkling bud of heaven
  That folds the heart of me.

On the deathless tree of Ygdrasil
  When the hymning tempest rings
My spirit rides the ranging boughs,
  And spreads his rainbow wings;
And down the lustrous whirlwind's breath,
  Where flaring comets stream,
He wafts that mystic merriment
  That wakes me when I dream.

Far on that golden-fruited Tree,
  In the everlasting rays
The spirit sits that whets my wits
  And glorifies my days:
Oh, scarce know I—mixed mud and sky,
  If bird or seraph he
Who lights me with that glittering eye
  In blue eternity.

                              James A. Mackereth.

THE CITY OF SLEEP

Manikin, maker of dreams,
  Came to the city of sleep:
The watch was on guard, and the gates were barred.
  And the moat was deep.

'Who is on my side, who?'
  Moonbeams rose in a row:
He tuned them loud betwixt town and cloud
  But his voice was low.

He sang a song of the moon
  For loan of her silver beams;
Misty and fair, and afloat in air,
  Lay the ladder of dreams.

He harped by river and hill;
  And the river forgot to flow,
And the wind in the grass forgot to pass,
  And the grass to grow.

He harped to the heart of earth
  Where honey in hive lies sweet:
And that sound leapt through the gates, and crept
  Through the silent street.

Manikin, maker of dreams,
    He pursed his lips to pipe:
And the strange and the new grew near and true,
    For the time was ripe.

He piped to the hearts of men:
    And dreamers rose up straight,
To drift unbarred by the drowsy guard,
    And beyond the gate.

He piped the dream of the maid:
    And her heart was up and away;
And fast it beat and hurried her feet
    To the gates of day.

He piped the dream of the mother,
    The cry of her babe for food:
And she rose from rest and gave it the breast
    And that was good!

He piped the dream of the child:
    And into its hands and feet
Came tunes to play of the live-long day;
    And that was sweet!

He piped to the heart of youth:
    And the heart of youth had sight
Of love to be won, and a race to be run;
    And that was right!

He piped the song of age:
    And that was a far-off song,—

When life made haste and the mouth could taste:—
But that was wrong!

Manikin, maker of dreams,
Had piped himself to sleep:
The watch was on guard, and the gates were barred,
And the moat was deep!

Laurence Housman.

THE LEADER

The sword fell down: I heard a knell;
    I thought that ease was best,
And sullen men that buy and sell
    Were host: and I was guest.
All unashamed I sat with swine,
    We shook the dice for war,
The night was drunk with an evil wine—
    But she went on before.

    She rode a steed of the sea-foam breed,
        All faery was her blade,
    And the armour on her tender limbs
        Was of the moonshine made.

By God that sends the master-maids,
    I know not whence she came,
But the sword she bore to save the soul
    Went up like an altar flame
Where a broken race in a desert place
    Call on the Holy Name.

    We strained our eyes in the dim day-rise,
        We could not see them plain;
    But two dead men from Valmy fen
        Rode at her bridle-rein.

I hear them all, my fathers call,
  I see them how they ride,
And where had been that rout obscene
  Was an army straight with pride.
A hundred thousand marching men,
  Of squadrons twenty score,
And after them all the guns, the guns,
  But she went on before.

> *Her face was like a king's command*
>   *When all the swords are drawn.*
> *She stretched her arms and smiled at us,*
> *Her head was higher than the hills.*
> *She led us on to endless plains.*
>   *We lost her in the dawn.*

Hilaire Belloc.

BALLAD OF THE SOUTH COUNTRY

To men who dwell in southern shires
  And breathe the air of down,
I'll tell a tale that few have heard
  In village or in town.

And he who listens while I tell,
  Here must he stand with me,
Where every wind that stirs the turf
  Must first have crossed the sea.

Long years ago, before the downs
  Became the curse of men,
There came a rider on his horse,
  And both were bold as ten.

They galloped right the length of down,
  And laughed, both man and beast:
Then sudden to the east-shore came,
  Yet recked not in the least,

But round they wheeled to right-about,
  With neither look nor jest,
And hence, and o'er our springy turf,
  Rode back towards the west.

And when they came to Ladyholt
  They laughed and turned again,

And wheeled about to right about,
  Not caring why or when.

And still they ride, to east, to west,
  The bare-backed slopes of down,
Though few have seen a man in green,
  Or horse of earthen brown.

But stand beside that golden patch
  Where flames the laughing gorse,
And tell me if you do not hear
  The gallop of a horse.

Some days you'll hear it coming aft,
  And sometimes on before,
From east to west, from west to east,
  Along the southern shore.

And who among our southern men
  Would glory in the down,
Must get astride and out and ride
  A steed of earthen brown.

                              E. A. Fielder.

ORIELDA

Sweet Orielda from the stars
  Stole down to earth again,
And burst the bright celestial bars,
  To ease a lover's pain.

She sought him by the woodland ways
  They once for trysting knew,
Where now, with sorrow all a-daze,
  He walked the dark night through.

The lovelight in her eyes did shine,
  She softly breathed his name,
And on his face a look divine
  Of joy seraphic came.

The Heaven from which her soul had sped
  Was very pure and high,
On earth they never could have wed—
  No more she wondered why.

What Orielda said that night
  I guess, but may not tell;
Brief words she spoke with presage bright
  Of all that soon befell.

At dawn they found her lover dead,
    In restful, radiant guise,
As one that on a happy bed
    Good dreams a-dreaming lies.

"Set free from strife and earthly jars!"
    They said, but none had spied
How Orielda from the stars
    Had kissed him as he died.

Oscar Boulton.

A DEAD POET

(James Elroy Flecker)

Weave for his brow the laurel wreath, he lies
For ever dumb, the lips that sang so well
Are locked in silence 'neath the alien skies,
And all the tales are told that he shall tell.

Ah, mourn a little, for his life was sweet,
And silence is too solemn after song,
He has gone hence ere men had time to greet
One who but seldom sang nor tarried long.

So sweet and light his singing, scarcely heard,
Only the silence touched our ears with sense
Of something void, as when a fluting bird
No more breaks on the valley's somnolence.

He has gone hence,—ah, whither! who shall say?
Perchance he treads the trackless paths of Night,
Long wearied in the Caravan of Day,
Perchance he seeks the Gardens of Delight,

And thro' dim-shaded valleys journeys on,
A moon-led pilgrim seeking for the Thing
Which dreamers spake of in the days long gone,
And poets sang of in a Grecian Spring.

It may be he has found those mounts of snow
All flushed with rose, those glades of endless sleep,
And knows the truths which many sought to know,
And wonders now why men grow sick and weep,

Why some are sad, as he was sad in days
When Beauty was too beautiful and frail,
When a dear voice was sweet beyond all praise,
Rising at night-time from a starlit vale.

O nevermore for him the sunset fades,
Nor ocean lifts her waters to the moon,
No more his feet shall wander in the glades,
His soul with mystic rapture deep aswoon;

For him no caravans with sound of bells
Move from the Syrian cities shadow-dim,
Nor long-lashed maidens dream by palm-girt wells,
Their phantom-world is all unknown to him.

He holds a wider converse with the stars,
And roams unfettered through the jewelled night,
His song flows in the wind 'mid nenuphars
Swaying and rustling in the dawning light.

Weave for his brow the laurel, for his name
What brighter memory than those sweet songs
Sung in a too-brief life that knew not fame,
Yet gave this wealth which now to Time belongs!

Cecil Roberts.

INDEX OF AUTHORS

217